Ritsos in Parentheses

THE LOCKERT LIBRARY OF POETRY IN TRANSLATION
EDITORIAL ADVISER, JOHN FREDERICK NIMS
FOR OTHER TITLES IN THE LOCKERT LIBRARY SEE PAGE 177

OTHER BOOKS BY EDMUND KEELEY

TRANSLATIONS

Six Poets of Modern Greece (with Philip Sherrard)
Vassilis Vassilikos: The Plant, the Well, the Angel (with Mary Keeley)
George Seferis: Collected Poems, 1924-1955 (with Philip Sherrard)
C. P. Cavafy: Passions and Ancient Days (with George Savidis)
C. P. Cavafy: Selected Poems (with Philip Sherrard)
Odysseus Elytis: The Axion Esti (with George Savidis)
C. P. Cavafy Collected Poems (with Philip Sherrard)
Angelos Sikelianos: Selected Poems (with Philip Sherrard)

NOVELS

The Libation
The Gold-Hatted Lover
The Impostor
Voyage to a Dark Island

CRITICISM

Modern Greek Writers (edited with Peter Bien)
Cavafy's Alexandria: Study of a Myth in Progress

Ritsos in Parentheses

TRANSLATIONS AND INTRODUCTION BY

Edmund Keeley

PRINCETON UNIVERSITY PRESS
PRINCETON, NEW JERSEY

Published by Princeton University Press, Princeton, New Jersey

Library of Congress Cataloging in Publication Data will be
found on the last printed page of this book

The Lockert Library of Poetry in Translation is supported by a bequest
from the late Lacy Lockert, scholar and translator of Corneille, Racine, and Dante

This book has been composed in V.I.P. Baskerville and Linotype Porson Greek

The Greek text of *Parentheses, 1946-47* and *The Distant* are based on the edition
published by Kedros, Athens, Greece. *Parentheses, 1950-61* is set from the poet's
manuscript

Clothbound editions of Princeton University Press books
are printed on acid-free paper, and binding materials are
chosen for strength and durability

Printed in the United States of America by Princeton
University Press, Princeton, New Jersey

For the members of the 1976-77 Translation Work-shop at Princeton, in gratitude for what they taught me about the tolerance, cunning, and devotion required by the art we explored together: Nadia Benabid, Caron Cadle, Doug McCloskey, Liz McGowan, Nancy Miller, Sam Moore, Merrell Noden, Madeleine Picciotto, Dolly Shaffer, and Patti Silver.

CONTENTS

The Distant

ACKNOWLEDGMENTS

I AM indebted to the Ingram Merrill Foundation and to the Princeton University Committee in the Humanities and Social Sciences for grants in support of this translation. I also want to thank Yannis Ritsos for his patient response to my queries—both of us assisted generously by Mary Keeley—during the summers of 1977 and 1978. Robert Fagles, Daniel Halpern, and Richard McKane offered several helpful suggestions regarding the translations, as did Paula DiPerna and Warren Wallace regarding the Introduction, and Robert Brown regarding the text in proof. Selections from this volume have appeared in *The New Yorker, Antaeus, The American Poetry Review, Boston University Journal, The Iowa Review, The Falcon, Field, Footprint Magazine, The Charioteer, Translation*, and *Pequod*.

INTRODUCTION

THE title I have given this selection of translations is not as playful as it may seem. Two of the three groups of poems by Ritsos from which the selection is made actually carry the title "Parentheses," the one written in 1946-47 and first published in volume two of the 1961 collected edition, the other covering poems written from 1950 to 1961 and still to be published in Greek. The third source, a volume called *The Distant*, written in 1975 and published in March 1977, was chosen by the poet to accompany these versions from the two "Parentheses" groups, presumably because he considers the poems from this recent volume to be in the same general mode as the earlier "parenthetical" works. It is in any case a consideration worth exploring, because the relation of this volume to its two predecessors, and the poet's development in mode and perspective between the three groups of poems, allow us to place his current voice in an illuminating context that seems to have been indicated by the poet himself.

In what sense are these three groups of poems from different periods "in parentheses"? They are not really an interlude between those longer works that were primarily responsible for shaping Ritsos's reputation in Greece—for example, "Epitaphios," "Romiosini," and "Moonlight Sonata"—because shorter poems of the kind found in these three groups have been important from the beginning and have now come to dominate Ritsos's oeuvre. One might call them parenthetical to those poems—early poems, on the whole—that promoted political themes directly and that helped to establish Ritsos as a leading Communist poet; but to regard them as an "aside" in this sense is to give too much weight to the ideological aspect of Ritsos's work and too much credit to his more blatantly political, rhetorical, and sometimes loquacious exercises. In my opinion, each of the three groups considered here reveals subtleties that are not found in more famous works, and though each group is uneven, the three combine to make a statement at least as important as that of any of the longer poems which served most to create Ritsos's reputation in his home country, in particular those that were assisted by the musical settings of Mikis Theodorakis.

My use of "parentheses" has more to do with metaphor than with judgment in any case. I am not sure what Ritsos himself has in mind when he offers the term, but certain metaphoric possibilities suggest themselves if "parentheses" are seen in the context of mathematics and symbolic logic, that is, as a way of designating separate groupings of symbols that form a unit or collective entity. The analogy underlines one aspect of these three groups of poems: a unity of symbolic vision or sensibility, both within the individual groups and progressively linking the three. Each shapes its own parenthesis, enclosing a particular way of viewing reality at a particular moment in the poet's career. At the same time, the three groupings, the three parentheses, are part of a developing vision that distinguishes these poems in terms of stance, mode, and perspective from other works—especially the longer ones—that make up Ritsos's vast oeuvre. The developing vision can be seen as an expansion of the space within the parenthesis representing each of the separate groups. In the case of each, the two signs of the parenthesis are like cupped hands facing each other across a distance, hands that are straining to come together, to achieve a meeting that would serve to reaffirm human contact between isolated presences; but though there are obvious gestures toward closing the gap between the hands, the gestures seem inevitably to fail, and the meeting never quite occurs. In terms of the poet's development, the distance within the parenthesis is shorter in each of the two earlier volumes. By the time we reach *The Distant* (the title especially significant in this context), the space between the cupped hands has become almost infinite, seemingly too vast for any ordinary human gesture that might try to bridge the parenthetical gap.

But before attempting to summarize the progress of the poet's vision, I want to consider the three groups in chronological order, using several representative poems from each to review the particular mode and perspective that distinguish the separate stages of Ritsos's development in these shorter works. The opening poem of *Parentheses, 1946-47*, "The Meaning of Simplicity," serves to introduce several of the poet's central preoccupations. The stance is that of a poet-persona who is hiding and who assumes that the reader will search to find him, will reach out to meet him and to touch if not his hand, at least his hand-print. A certain distance is taken for granted—the gap within a parenthesis, if you will—and at least the possibility of a failure to meet. But also taken for granted at this stage is the necessity of the attempt. The poem reads almost as though it were a credo: "Like Cavafy, I can be understood only from hidden things, but the things I hide behind are simple, and there is access to them through words when the words are true. Reader, try to find me through my words, because I want a meeting, no matter how difficult it may be for us to reach each other—in fact, I insist on the meeting."

This poem is one of the very few seemingly personal statements among the twenty-one that make up *Parentheses, 1946-47*. The first-person voice does not appear again until the last poem in the volume; between the first and the last we find poems that make use of the second person, the third person, first-person plural, second-person plural, any grammatical strategy for avoiding the simple "I" of lyrical or subjective statement, further evidence of the poet's impulse to hide, in this regard behind an objective stance.

The best poems in this volume are those that offer a dramatic context to supplement Ritsos's calculated—not to say programmatic—objectivity in mode of narration. The best poems are also far from simple, for all their apparent focus on relatively simple things. "Miniature" is a case in point, among the subtlest and finest of the many hundred shorter poems that Ritsos has written. The simple things in this poem are an unidentified woman, an unidentified officer, some thin slices of lemon, an old armchair, a match, a cigarette, a teacup. And the action is really an absence of action: a visit that could lead to a meeting of some kind, a coming together that finally does not take place. Yet what a complex miniature drama it is. And those simple slices of lemon become a beautifully complicated metaphor that is the heart of the poem. The woman and the young officer face each other across their basic furniture with some expectation in their undefined relationship, enough expectation anyway to keep the visitor from looking at the woman and to make his hand tremble as it holds the match. Is it a purely erotic possibility, a potential meeting of lovers at the most fundamental level? It would hardly seem so when those simple slices of lemon that the woman's sad hands are preparing for tea shape a small carriage that invokes a distant fairy-tale world of childhood and, by extension, the mother-son aspect of this encounter between a woman of unidentified age and an officer specifically designated as young, with a "tender chin." In any case, before this ambiguous expectation of love can be realized, the clock holds its heartbeat for a moment, time is suspended, then the meeting at whatever level is postponed, and the moment of possible touching, whether physical or emotional or both, passes and is gone. And in its passing, the lemon-slice carriage of a child's fairy tale is replaced by an invisible carriage bearing death. The death of the moment's possibilities? The death of such ambiguous expectations? Or more literally, a foreshadowing of the officer's death in battle and the doom of any future for him (these poems written between 1946 and 1947 sometimes give strong hints of the larger historical context, the ruthless civil war, that the dates of their composition evoke)?

The several questions raised by the poem are beyond simple things, and the poem implies each question without offering a precise answer to any one. We know only that the carriage bearing death has come and gone in the moment of mystery when the clock stopped its heartbeat, that the expectation of more than a meeting over tea has been postponed, that it is now too late for a consummation of this trembling encounter between woman and man sometimes playing mother and son. There can be no further challenge to death now, temporary or otherwise. Their attention returns to the tea table, left now with only that lemon-wheel carriage parked on its unlit side street—its street of lost hopes and impossible expectations, perhaps—and soon not even that but the dwindling life of a song diminishing to a little mist and then to nothing.

The poem that follows "Miniature" in *Parentheses, 1946-47*, "Women," is one of the two selected from this volume for inclusion in George Veloudis's recent "chronological anthology" of Ritsos—preferred, I suppose, because the surface of it has an immediate appeal that seems to place it closer than others to what is normally regarded as the mainstream of Ritsos's verse, at least that current in it having to do with the poor and their burdens. But below the surface there are further subtle strategies and ambiguities that link this poem to the previous one and to others that show us failed gestures which are meant to establish some contact between more or less isolated people, failed attempts to break out of loneliness or aloneness and—in terms of our metaphor—to shorten the distance that separates the two cupped hands that face each other in a parenthesis. The title is generic, and so is the opening line: "Women are very distant." It is not "the" woman of the previous poem or of later poems where the definite article serves to make the term almost purely symbolic. To begin with, it is women in general who are distant, whose sheets put one off with the kind of "good night" that suggests a turning of the back—and this use of the generic term itself establishes distance, impersonality, as does the responding "we" of the second line, an attempt by the poet initially to bring us into this conspiracy of gestures, the first of which suggests rejection by "women" but which is soon followed by a gesture on their part that seems an attempt to fill the distance, the gap between "them" and "us": "they set bread on the table" so that their absence is less painful to us. And we respond with a like gesture by offering to light the lamp, because we recognize our role in the creation of this distance: "it was our fault." As we strike the match, women in general suddenly become a single, more personal "she," turning away from our gesture with a bitter burden of death on her back, including, unnervingly, "your own."

By the end of the second stanza not only has there been a grammatical movement from the general to the more personal in the woman's case, but the first-person plural identifying the general male protagonist has shifted to the second-person singular, again a grammatical gesture toward the more personal, one that now includes not only a more specific protagonist but the reader as well, the "hypocrite lecteur," if you will. Then, as the woman turns away again and moves farther into her private world of sorrow where the dishes cry in the rack, you—you, me, and the poet's persona—see that her sorrow is perhaps not so personal as we have begun to take for granted, occasioned not so much by our role in her life and our failed gestures or even by the family dead and our own death that she bears as by the fate of those soldiers on their way to the front and by the woman's symbolic role as grieving lover, wife, mother to them all—what we carry to this poem from the ambiguous confrontation in the poem that precedes it. The allusion to the soldiers on their way to battle has turned the rhythm of our little drama right back to the general context from which it started and from which the poet's subtle grammatical gesturing in the second stanza seemed about to save us. Women *are* very distant in the end, and they have good reason to be, given the tragic roles we and the times force them to play. And that distance, though bridged occasionally by gestures on both their part and ours, seems as sadly inevitable and inexorable by the time we reach the last line as the poet suggested it was in the first.

My bringing into the discussion of this poem implications established in the previous one may appear arbitrary, but it is consistent with the poet's mode in these poems, which is to build a collective statement through the repetition of related motifs from one poem to another, a mode that becomes even more obvious and dramatic in its effect in Ritsos's latest collections. A few lines from other poems in the volume will illustrate the collective aspect of one central theme we have been exploring, that of the lonely or alone aspiring, and usually failing, to meet another isolated presence, and with the failure, sometimes settling for self-sufficiency. From "Maybe, Someday": "But I'm going to insist on seeing and showing you, he said, / because if you too don't see, it will be as if I hadn't— / I'll insist at least on not seeing with your eyes— / and maybe someday, from a different direction, we'll meet"; from a poem called "Self-sufficiency?": "Under the trees two chairs. Why two? / Ah yes, one to sit on, one for stretching your legs"; from "Understanding": ". . . To be able to look / outside yourself—warmth and peacefulness. Not to be / 'only you' but 'you too' . . ."; and from "The Same Star": "That man suspects that in every mirror / there's another, transparent woman, locked in her nakedness / —much as you may want to wake her, she won't wake up. / She fell asleep smelling a star. / And he lies awake smelling that same star."

It would be hard to argue for the same kind of thematic coherence in the case of *Parentheses, 1950-61*, which is really a sampling from a larger group of unpublished poems written over a much longer period of time. Yet there are related preoccupations and strategies in this second group, as the poet's choice of title emphasizes. Failure of contact and recourse to self-sufficiency are there again in one of the few first-person exercises, a rather wry little poem called "A Wreath," where the isolated persona decides to crown himself with a wreath made of the leaves that have successfully kept him from finding the person he has been trying to reach. A more insistent theme is that of our failure to cope with the realities of both civilization and nature, of our being at a loss in an environment that does not comprehend our sometimes misdirected or awkward intentions—and I say "our" because this theme

is usually expressed in the first-person plural, presumably in order
to establish a more general relevance and again to solicit the
reader's complicity. In "Delay" we find ourselves arriving late at the
theatre—"we're always late"—stumbling over the knees and the in-
sentient feet of an ugly old woman, suddenly feeling that we're the
ones on stage because the lights go on and the clapping seems di-
rected at us. And in "Message," the message has clearly not gotten
through to us that nature is preparing for planting and rebirth
while we go on putting in a heating stove and ignoring the obvious
signs of blue skies ahead: the plumber's blue overalls, the new pipes
shining like the trunks of trees, and most of all, the sturdy blue
eggs that the chickens have begun to lay beside the wine barrel and
the plough.

But the most persistent theme in this group focuses not on our
misdirected actions that seem to go contrary to nature or on our
stumbling attempts to find our place in a perverse environment but
on our not being able to act at all or on our obsession with things
that don't happen and places that are empty and closed. One poem
is called "Inertia"; another is called "He Who Didn't Dance." And
in "The Only," it isn't enough that what has been anticipated for
some time doesn't in fact happen—the "what" never even identified—but those who have anticipated something happening find, as
they take the flags down, that they are left with only one prop to
sustain them in place of action, only one substitute for the once ex-
pected but now missing barbarian solution in this neo-Cavafian
world: the lack of any excuse. In the same poem we learn that "the
walls smell strongly of unfamiliarity," as well they might in such
alienated circumstances. At other times in *Parentheses, 1950-61*, the
surroundings smell of emptiness, of absence, of the wrong season,
because, as "Autumn Expression" puts it, "The great dampness has
set in. The vacationers have left." From "Desk Calendar" we learn
that "everyone has gone abroad" in midwinter, leaving us with
"Desperate gestures by the wind / in front of the closed hotel's glass
door."

Ritsos doesn't designate precise sources or reasons for the sense
of dislocation and absence, of inertia and silence, that pervade the
landscape he paints in this second group of poems, nor does he
offer clear indication of what might bring about a change in his
country of suspended possibilities and aborted expectations—a

stance here and elsewhere that gives the lie to his being simply a propagandist for extreme political solutions, as he was sometimes accused of being by the Greek literary establishment during the fifties (when he was acknowledged at all). The only clue we have to his vision of the future, of the way things may turn, in this admittedly incomplete image of his perspective during the decade emerges from two of the more substantial and complicated poems in *Parentheses, 1950-61*, both of which suggest the possible advent of new gods to replace the old—and a new attitude toward gods however defined—in Ritsos's contemporary landscape. The first, "In the Ruins of an Ancient Temple," places the old and the new in direct juxtaposition: "The museum guard was smoking in front of the sheepfold. / The sheep were grazing among the marble ruins." One might be tempted to see the poem as simply an ironic treatment of the relation between antiquity and a modern sensibility, a kind of mock pastoral, say: the shepherd and even the guard seem to accept the ancient marble ruins as ordinary, everyday objects in their bucolic landscape, as though the ruins have been drained by time of any godly association whatsoever and are now as much a part of this world as the very earthly sheep gamboling among them—in fact, at one point sheep and ruins cannot be distinguished from each other: ". . . The sheep ran to him / as though the marble ruins were running." And the woman with her washing, of the first stanza—I suppose the best that we can get for a nymph in this modern landscape—is wonderfully casual toward the ancient gods, not to say downright sacrilegious, in hanging her husband's underpants on Hera's shoulders. Also, in the second stanza, in place of the old procession honoring a goddess, we have fishermen with baskets full of flashing, multicolored fish—even worse, the goddess's richly embroidered veil has been cut up to make curtains and tablecloths. But is it really worse? Is the poet's stance ironic? The poem seems to offer a contrary, anyway an ambivalent, implication: there may be good reason for these new primitives to submit to practical necessity when the old gods have lost their godly relevance and when the houses people are supposed to live in have been emptied. Rather than simple irony, one gets the sense of territory being cleared—or more to the point, of air being cleared—for new beginnings. In treating the ancient gods so casually, with such familiarity, in turning them from agents of mystery into useful domestic objects as necessity demands, these inhabitants of a modern pastoral world seem not only to have accommodated their ancient past but to have neutralized it, as though preparing for new gods, as though preparing perhaps to start the divine cycle over again in terms of the contemporary reality they actually live, even if their new or redefined gods prove less marble-constant and accessible.

This interpretation would appear to gain some support from the second poem specifically having to do with gods, "Incense," in particular the concluding lines, where lighting up a cigarette is seen as a new kind of divine ritual (we may have been prepared for this by the persistent smoking in Ritsos's poems, as in his workshop) and where cigarette smoke—joining that from the houses with some rooms still closed—becomes the new incense. What is the god now honored, at least in memory? One unknown, unapproachable, designated as "entirely their own" (to distinguish him, presumably, from gods belonging to others, to the old tradition, to enemies, whoever they may be exactly)—a god otherwise unnamed and undefined. That this god is acknowledged on the threshold of partially closed space and that he is unapproachable does not come as a surprise, given the themes we have already encountered in this group of poems. At the same time, it *is* on a threshold that the men seem to remember him, and they are in the process of emerging from the closed, glassed-in quarters of the first stanza into the open air on their way to work, suggesting, perhaps, that it is a new hearth-god their smoke has signaled. That is as much as the poem offers in the way of a prospect for the future, and given both the god's attributes and the merely hypothetical evocation of him, it is an equivocal prospect at best.

By the time we reach *The Distant*, written some fifteen years after the last of the poems we have been considering, Ritsos's landscape has taken on a harshness and a bleakness beyond anything manifest in the earlier works, yet there is new power in the way this latest phase of his vision is projected. The reigning deity has become, as the title poem suggests, the embodiment of distance, silence, the unapproachable, inaction—all that *Parentheses, 1950-61* implied but that has now arrived at an ultimate extreme. Though the title poem is the last in the volume, it has the tone of an invocation, anyway a prayer to a god who has hovered in the wings of

Ritsos's parenthetical world for some years and who is here brought onto center stage to be openly hymned: "O distant, distant; deep unapproachable; receive always / the silent ones in their absence, in the absence of the others / when the danger from the near ones, from the near itself, burdens / during nights of promise. . . ." The gap separating the two hands of our metaphorical parenthesis seems to have widened almost to infinity if the most tangible danger is that from "the near ones, from the near itself," and if that which serves to shore up the world, as we learn later in the poem, is a thing that cannot be granted, a thing without obligations, living invisibly in the realm of inaction where music reigns. One might be tempted to see the reference to music as a positive sign, evidence of a saving lyrical transcendence in this country of bleak absolutes dominated by distance, silence, and the unapproachable; but the concrete "things" and characters that make up the down-to-earth landscape of these poems allow only the smallest space for this possibility of relief, at least as my eye sees the poetic territory that Ritsos shows us in this volume, after fifteen years of cruel history on both a national and personal level, including the poet's second period of imprisonment and exile, from 1967 to 1969, under the colonels.

Most of the elements that build the new landscape in *The Distant* are familiar from earlier poems, but they are presented in this volume in a style that has been purified of all decoration and that finds its strength in a renewed commitment to simplicity and economy (to paraphrase George Seferis's parallel ambition): no overt sentiment, no obvious metaphors, the syntax basic, the colors primary—if sometimes perverse—the details focused with precision to create a startling image of a country haunted by secret violence:

The deep voice was heard in the deeper night.
Then the tanks went by. Then day broke.
Then the voice was heard again, shorter, farther in.
The wall was white. The bread red. The ladder
rested almost vertical against the antique lamppost. The old
  woman
collected the black stones one by one in a paper bag.

The action in this poem, called "Toward Saturday," is also treated with economy, just the bare facts and no commentary: a deep voice

in the night, tanks going by, an old woman collecting stones (in con-
trast, one assumes, to gathering wood for warmth or wild greens
for food—but the poet doesn't say so). It is a powerfully rendered
landscape of bad dreams, of remembered horror, with dangers
and threats that remain unresolved but that are no less real for it.
And if it evokes nightmares occasioned by the Greek dictatorship
of 1967 to 1974 or earlier harsh history in Greece, it does not need
that kind of local, topical definition to engender a strong response,
because the images reach more broadly into the shared psychic
consciousness of our times.

Perhaps the central figure in this nightmare landscape is a
trapped victim trying to hide from unexplained forces, enemies
identified only as "they" and "them": "He heard them calling his
name over the water. / He verified that it was for him. He hid."
(from "Secretly"). And when the unidentified "they" dig the victim
out of hiding, as they surely must, they mock those gestures by him
that establish his humanity:

RED-HANDED

Throw the spotlight right on his face;
hidden like this in the night, let's see him, make him glow;
he has beautiful teeth—and he knows it; he smiles
with the small moon up on the bombed-out hill,
with the children of the woodcutters down by the river.

The threat of arrest and annihilation pursues the nightmare victim
even in those moments that should be exhilarating, joyous, as in
"Preparing the Ceremony," where the persona, about to be celebrated at a public gathering in a large hall, not only finds that he's
suddenly missing but also realizes that if he were somehow to redis-
cover himself and get his feet to move, the usher would arrest him.

The victim's loss of contact with himself is paralleled by a total
loss of contact with others in those poems that pick up the theme of
two people confronting each other in some attempt at dialogue.
The essential dialogue has now moved farther away from a meeting through words, as the title of one poem, "Brief Dialogue," underlines, and even the bed where it is conducted is seen by the
woman in the same poem as "a silent fierce animal getting ready to
leave." The distance separating the "he" and "she" in this volume

appears unbridgeable. They are dead to each other—literally so, it would seem, in "Completeness Almost," even if their dialogue strives to deny it: "You know, death doesn't exist, he said to her. / I know, yes, now that I'm dead, she answered." At best they confront each other as suspicious cripples, seeing one another in the reflection from a glass eye, again literally:

COURT EXHIBIT

The woman was still lying on the bed. He
took out his glass eye, set it down on the table,
took a step, stopped. Now do you believe me? he said to her.
She picked up the glass eye, brought it close to her eye; she
    looked at him.

That final look is the one touch of ambiguity the poet allows himself, though the general context of these poems leads us to suspect that the "exhibit" does not really convince the lady in the end.

The one poem that actually offers an image of physical contact, the three handsome young men linked shoulder to shoulder in "Winter Sunshine," tells us, parenthetically, that the one in the middle is a statue; and the three are seen to be strolling "in the sun-lit insouciance of death." The theme, the death of meetings once assumed possible and necessary, finds its logical conclusion in "With the Unapproachable," where the "he" makes what seems an ultimate commitment to self-sufficiency: "So very very distant— and therefore invulnerable too—he said; / yet no one distant enough; no one as much as he would like, / as much maybe as he could be or should be."

The perspective of these poems—unsentimental, at times almost dehumanized, at times dryly harsh, yet in touch with a felt reality—emerges in its boldest outlines if we read the poems in sequence, because here, as in the earlier volumes, the poems build on each other to shape a composite statement, one that is even more coherent and unified, if also at times more disturbing, than those of the two *Parentheses*, one that is characteristic in its density and mode of several of Ritsos's most recent volumes. The interconnected attitudes, characters, and objects in *The Distant* create the kind of general image a poetic novella might offer, though without a plot and without transitions to bind the structure together. The binding is the poet's relentless vision. And the reappearance of persistent motifs works to establish a symbolic landscape that gradually becomes familiar. The elements taken by themselves may sometimes seem obscurely personal—what do the old woman's black stones represent exactly, or the recurring statues, the mirrors, the walls, the bread, etc.?—but on reading the volume through, and especially on rereading the volume through, these individual "things" begin to fall into a context, until we see them as thoroughly at home, as inevitable, in the strange new wasteland world the poet has constructed. It is a world inhabited on the whole by people who are old or crippled or dead, both figuratively and literally—the one-eyed, the one-armed, the petrified, the missing, those on the way to burial—a world in which nature has been drained of normal sustenance. Yet a struggle to survive, whether by hiding or by establishing a protective distance or by trying out new rituals, continues in at least some measure among these victims of undefined enemies. In "Reconstruction" (as positive a title as one is likely to find in late Ritsos) some of the individual symbols come together with unusual force to shape an especially arid image of the poet's imagined country, territory where there is no earth, where no grass grows, only stones, rafters, a burnt tree, and the burden of death again. Yet we find in the same poem a new, unexpected ritual that seems meant to rejuvenate the landscape and to reaffirm some possibility of contact between the tortured inhabitants of Ritsos's wasteland, a ritual that brings the inhabitants again in touch with the earth, the soil, as well as with each other (significantly, shoeless feet replace hands as the agents of this new attempt at a meeting) and that ends—very much in the Greek tradition—with a dance:

> Then we lit the great fires; we set the old man on the rock;
> we took off our boots; and sitting like this on the ground
> two by two we measured our feet, soles against soles.
> Young Konstandis, who had the largest feet, danced first.

The poet's thirty-year journey from *Parentheses, 1946-47* to *The Distant* has been one of bitter catharsis, a progress from his focus on so-called simple things and more or less abortive gestures to a focus on bare—not to say barren—essentials and primitive rituals performed by those whose deity appears to be an infinitely distant, absolutely white, unapproachable and silent ambiguity. The starkness of this late vision, with its desiccated landscape and haunting presence of death, is paralleled by an aesthetic absoluteness that replaces the earlier grammatical complexity with an uncomplicated syntax consisting largely of declarative sentences and a purified style that leaves no room for figures of speech, no coloring other than basic adjectives, no images that have not been drained of overt sentiment. It has been a movement from masked simplicity to an attempt at the real thing. The earlier mode produced poems of subtlety and warmth, and it also produced poems marred by sentimentality; the later mode precludes sentimentality, but it does not always preclude an excess of stylistic dryness and a degree of obscurity. Yet the effect of the long catharsis in those late poems that work well is to provide a sense of reality that transcends the merely representational, a sense of the deeper psychic meanings—the hidden threats and nightmare memories—that lie below the surface of things. The poet's development has served to promote symbolic richness at the expense of decorative coloring and tragic vision at the expense of ideological rhetoric.

The development starts much earlier than has been generally acknowledged in Greek literary circles—as we have seen, at least as early as the best of *Parentheses, 1946-47*. Beginning with that volume, Ritsos appears to have moved in much the same direction as that chosen by his strongest predecessors in this century, Cavafy, Sikelianos, and Seferis. Each abandoned rhetorical self-indulgence or subjective lyricism at some point in his career in favor of the dramatic and symbolic expression of a tragic sense of life that came to each with a mature vision of the human predicament and that discovered its profoundest form in the kind of simplicity which emerges from catharsis, personal and stylistic. These three groups of poems "in parentheses" can be taken as testimony of both the pain and the wisdom of Ritsos's progress toward a like discovery.

Parentheses, 1946-47

Πίσω ἀπὸ ἁπλὰ πράγματα κρύβομαι, γιὰ νὰ μὲ βρεῖτε·
ἂν δὲ μὲ βρεῖτε, θὰ βρεῖτε τὰ πράγματα,
θ' ἀγγίξετε ἐκεῖνα ποὺ ἄγγιξε τὸ χέρι μου,
θὰ σμίξουν τὰ χνάρια τῶν χεριῶν μας.

Τὸ αὐγουστιάτικο φεγγάρι γυαλίζει στὴν κουζίνα
σὰ γανωμένο τεντζέρι (γι' αὐτὸ ποὺ σᾶς λέω γίνεται ἔτσι)
φωτίζει τ' ἄδειο σπίτι καὶ τὴ γονατισμένη σιωπὴ τοῦ
    σπιτιοῦ —
πάντα ἡ σιωπὴ μένει γονατισμένη.

Ἡ κάθε λέξη εἶναι μιὰ ἔξοδος
γιὰ μιὰ συνάντηση, πολλὲς ψορὲς ματαιωμένη,
καὶ τότε εἶναι μιὰ λέξη ἀληθινή, σὰν ἐπιμένει στὴ συνάντηση.

I hide behind simple things so you'll find me;
if you don't find me, you'll find the things,
you'll touch what my hand has touched,
our hand-prints will merge.

The August moon glitters in the kitchen
like a tin-plated pot (it gets that way because of what I'm saying to
     you),
it lights up the empty house and the house's kneeling silence—
always the silence remains kneeling.

Every word is a doorway
to a meeting, one often cancelled,
and that's when a word is true: when it insists on the meeting.

Πέρασε ἡ νύχτα μπουκωμένη ἀμίλητο νερό. Τὰ χαράματα
ἔλαμψε ὁ ἥλιος μουσκεμένος στὰ κουλουριασμένα
    καραβόσκοινα.
Πρόσωπα - σκιές, κατάρτια - σκιές, ταξίδια —
τἄδαμε, δὲν τἄδαμε — δὲ χόρτασε ἡ πείνα μας.

Κάποιος φώναζε πίσω ἀπ᾽ τὸ βουνό· κάποιος ἄλλος
πίσω ἀπ᾽ τὰ δέντρα· κ᾽ ἕνας ἄλλος κι ἄλλος
σ᾽ ὅλο τὸ μάκρος τοῦ δειλινοῦ — ποῦ νὰ τρέξουμε;
Ποῦ νὰ προφτάσουμε; Μήπως εἴμαστε ἐμεῖς ποὺ φωνάζαμε;
    Καὶ τὰ βουνὰ
γίνονταν πιὸ μεγάλα καὶ κοφτερὰ σὰν τὰ δόντια τοῦ
    πεινασμένου.

The night went by with its mouth full of speechless water. At
    daybreak
the sun shone drenched on the coiled lines.
Face-shadows, mast-shadows, voyages—
we barely saw them—our hunger wasn't satisfied.

Somebody was shouting behind the mountain; somebody else
behind the trees; somebody else again, and again
the full length of the sunset—where should we run?
Which way first? Could we be the ones who were shouting? And the
    mountains
grew larger and sharper like the teeth of the one who hungered.

Εἶναι ἕνα πρόσωπο φωτεινό, σιωπηλό, καταμόναχο
σὰν ὁλόκληρη μοναξιά, σὰν ὁλόκληρη νίκη
πάνω στὴ μοναξιά. Αὐτὸ τὸ πρόσωπο
σὲ κοιτάζει ἀνάμεσα ἀπὸ δυὸ στῆλες ἀσάλευτο νερό.

Καὶ δὲ γνωρίζεις ποιό ἀπ’ τὰ δυὸ σὲ πείθει περισσότερο.

It's a lucid face, silent, entirely alone
like total solitude, like total victory
over solitude. This face
looks at you between two columns of still water.

And you don't know which of the two persuades you most.

Τὰ τέσσερα παράθυρα κρεμοῦν στὶς κάμαρες
ὁμοιοκατάληκτα τετράστιχα ἀπὸ οὐρανὸ καὶ θάλασσα.
Μιὰ παπαρούνα μόνη εἶναι ἕνα ρολογάκι
στὸ χέρι τοῦ καλοκαιριοῦ, νὰ δείχνει
δώδεκα ἡ ὥρα μεσημέρι. Κ' ἔτσι νιώθεις
τὰ μαλλιά σου πιασμένα μὲς στὰ δάχτυλα τοῦ ἥλιου
νὰ σὲ κρατᾶνε ἐλεύθερο μέσα στὸ φῶς καὶ στὸν ἀέρα.

The four windows hang rhyming quatrains
of sky and sea in the rooms.
A lone poppy is a watch
on the wrist of summer, telling
the hour of twelve noon. And so you feel
your hair caught up in the sun's fingers
holding you free in the light and the wind.

Θέλω νὰ σοῦ δείξω αὐτὰ τὰ ρόδινα σύννεφα μέσα στὴ νύχτα.
Μὰ ἐσὺ δὲ βλέπεις. Εἶναι νύχτα — τί νὰ δεῖς;

Λοιπόν, μοῦ μένει νὰ κοιτάξω μὲ τὰ μάτια σου, εἶπε,
γιὰ νὰ μὴν εἶμαι μόνος, νὰ μὴν εἶσαι μόνος. Κι ἀλήθεια,
δὲν εἶναι τίποτα πρὸς τὰ ἐκεῖ ὅπου σοῦ ἔδειχνα.

Τ' ἀστέρια μόνο στριμωγμένα μὲς στὴ νύχτα, κουρασμένα
σὰν τοὺς ἐκδρομεῖς ποὺ γυρνᾶνε μ' ἕνα φορτηγὸ
μετανιωμένοι, νυσταγμένοι, δίχως νὰ τραγουδᾶνε,
μὲ τ' ἀγριολούλουδα μαραμένα στὶς ἱδρωμένες παλάμες τους.

Μὰ ἐγὼ θὰ ἐπιμείνω νὰ δῶ καὶ νὰ σοῦ δείξω, εἶπε,
γιατὶ ἂν δὲ δεῖς κ' ἐσὺ θἆναι σὰ νὰ μὴν εἶδα —
θὰ ἐπιμείνω τουλάχιστο νὰ μὴ βλέπω μὲ τὰ μάτια σου —
κ' ἴσως μιὰ μέρα, ἀπ' ἄλλο δρόμο, νὰ συναντηθοῦμε.

I want to show you these rose clouds in the night.
But you don't see. It's night—what can one see?

Now, I have no choice but to see with your eyes, he said,
so I'm not alone, so you're not alone. And really,
there's nothing over there where I pointed.

Only the stars crowded together in the night, tired,
like those people coming back in a truck from a picnic,
disappointed, hungry, nobody singing,
with wilted wildflowers in their sweaty palms.

But I'm going to insist on seeing and showing you, he said,
because if you too don't see, it will be as if I hadn't—
I'll insist at least on not seeing with your eyes—
and maybe someday, from a different direction, we'll meet.

Τοῦτο τὸ πρωϊνὸ ἔχει φορτωθεῖ στὴ ράχη του τὸν ἥλιο
ἀνηφορίζοντας τοὺς ἀττικοὺς λοφίσκους
σὰν ἕνα παλληκάρι φορτωμένο μὲ τὸ ἀκορντεόν του.

Πάει κ᾽ ἡ νύχτα ἡ χτεσινὴ μὲ τὴ χαρά της,
καὶ μὲ τὸ φόβο της γιὰ τὴ χαρά της. Πάει
κ᾽ ἡ λύπη ἐκείνη ποὺ δὲν ἔλπιζε στὸ τέλος της.

Τὰ πεῦκα, ὁ ἥλιος, τὰ παράθυρα — καὶ τὰ βλέπουμε.
Κάτω ἀπ᾽ τὰ δέντρα δυὸ καρέκλες. Γιατί δύο;
Ἄ, ναί, ἡ μιὰ νὰ καθήσεις, ἡ ἄλλη ν᾽ ἀπλώσεις τὰ πόδια σου.

This particular morning has taken the sun on its back
climbing the Attic hills
like a young man loaded with his accordion.

Gone is last night with its pleasure,
and with its fear of its pleasure. Gone too
that sadness that had no hope of ending.

The pine trees, the sun, the windows—there they are.
Under the trees two chairs. Why two?
Ah yes, one to sit on, one for stretching your legs.

Ὅταν ἡ βροχὴ χτύπησε τὸ τζάμι μὲ τὄνα της δάχτυλο,
τὸ παράθυρο ἄνοιξε πρὸς τὰ μέσα. Στὸ βάθος
ἕνα ἄγνωστο πρόσωπο, ἕνας ἦχος — ἡ δική σου φωνή;
Ἡ φωνή σου δυσπιστοῦσε στ' αὐτί σου. Τὴν ἄλλη μέρα
ὁ ἥλιος κατηφόριζε στὰ χωράφια, σὰ μιὰ κάθοδος
ἀγροτῶν μὲ δρεπάνια καὶ δικράνια. Βγῆκες κ' ἐσὺ στὸ δρόμο
φωνάζοντας, χωρὶς νὰ ξέρεις τί φωνάζεις,
σταματώντας μιὰ στιγμὴ μ' ἕνα χαμόγελο κάτω ἀπ' τὴ φωνή
    σου
σὰν κάτω ἀπ' τὴ ρόδινη, ὁλόφωτη ὀμπρέλα μιᾶς γυναίκας
ποὺ σεργιάνιζε μπρὸς στὸ κιγκλίδωμα τοῦ πάρκου.
Ἐκεῖ ἀναγνώρισες ἀπρόοπτα πὼς αὐτὴ εἶταν ἡ σωστή σου
    φωνὴ
σύμφωνα μ' ὅλες τὶς ἀνύποπτες φωνὲς ποὺ γέμιζαν τὸν ἀέρα.

When the rain struck the windowpane with one of its fingers,
the window opened inward. At the far end
an unknown face, a sound—your voice?
Your voice distrusted your ear. The next day
the sun climbed down the fields, like a descent
of farmers with sickles and pitchforks. You came out into the road
shouting, not knowing what you were shouting,
stopping a moment with a smile under your voice
as under the pink, radiant umbrella of a woman
sauntering along the railing of a park.
There you recognized abruptly that this was your true voice
in accord with all the unsuspecting voices filling the air.

Αὐτὸ ποὺ λὲς γαλήνη ἢ πειθαρχία, καλοσύνη ἢ ἀπάθεια,
αὐτὸ ποὺ λὲς κλεισμένο στόμα μὲ σφιγμένα δόντια
δείχνοντας τὴ γλυκειὰ σιωπὴ τοῦ στόματος, κρύβοντας τὰ
    σφιγμένα δόντια,
εἶναι μονάχα ἡ καρτερία τῶν μετάλλων κάτω ἀπ' τὸ χρήσιμο
    σφυρί,
κάτω ἀπ' τὸ τρομερὸ σφυρὶ — εἶναι ποὺ ξέρεις
πῶς ἀπ' τὸ ἄμορφο περνᾶς πρὸς τὴ μορφή.

What you call peacefulness or discipline, kindness or apathy,
what you call a shut mouth with teeth clenched,
indicating the mouth's sweet silence, hiding the clenched teeth,
is only the patient endurance of metal under the useful hammer,
under the terrible hammer—is your knowledge
that you're moving from formlessness toward form.

Σιωπηλὴ νύχτα. Σιωπηλή. Κ' εἶχες πάψει
νὰ περιμένεις. Εἶταν ἤσυχα σχεδόν.
Καὶ ξαφνικὰ στὸ πρόσωπό σου τόσο ἔντονη
ἡ ἀφὴ κείνου ποὺ λείπει. Θἄρθει. Τότε ἀκούστηκε
ποὺ χτύπησαν μονάχα τὰ παραθυρόφυλλα.
Ἔβαλε ἀγέρα. Καὶ πιὸ κάτω ἡ θάλασσα
πνιγόταν μὲς στὴν ἴδια τὴ φωνή της.

Quiet night. Quiet. And you had stopped
waiting. It was peaceful almost.
And suddenly on your face the touch, so vivid,
of the one who is absent. He'll come. Then
the sound of shutters banging on their own.
Now the wind has come up. And a little farther, the sea
was drowning in its own voice.

Νυχτερινὸ ἱπποδρόμιο, τὰ φῶτα, ἡ μουσική,
τ' ἀστραφτερὰ αὐτοκίνητα σ' ὅλο τὸ μάκρος τῆς λεωφόρου.
Ὅταν σβήνουν τὰ φῶτα στὴ συνοικία,
ὅταν κ' ἡ τελευταία νότα πέφτει σὰν ξερὸ φύλλο,
ἡ πρόσοψη τοῦ ἱπποδρομίου γίνεται
σὰν πελώρια βγαλμένη μασέλλα. Τότε
τὰ χάλκινα ὄργανα κοιμοῦνται στὶς θῆκες τους,
πάνω ἀπ' τὴν πολιτεία ἀκούγεται ἡ κραυγὴ τῶν ζώων,
ἡ τίγρις μέσα στὸ κλουβί της προσηλώνεται στὸν ἴσκιο της,
ὁ θηριοδαμαστὴς βγάζει τὴ στολή του καὶ καπνίζει τὸ
    τσιγάρο του.

Κ' ἡ συνοικία στιγμὲς - στιγμὲς φωτίζεται
καθὼς ἀστράφτουν τὰ μάτια τῶν λιονταριῶν πίσω ἀπ' τὰ
    κάγκελα.

Night circus, the lights, the music,
the sparkling cars along the full length of the avenue.
When the lights go out in the neighborhood,
when the last note has fallen like a dry leaf,
the façade of the circus seems
a huge set of false teeth. Then
the brass instruments sleep in their cases,
the animals are heard bellowing over the city,
the tiger in its cage fixes on its own shadow,
the animal-tamer takes off his costume and smokes a cigarette.

And every now and then the neighborhood lights up
when the eyes of the lions sparkle behind their bars.

Τὸ ἀπόγευμα εἶναι ὅλο πεσμένους σουβάδες, μαῦρες πέτρες,
    ξερὰ ἀγκάθια.
Τὸ ἀπόγευμα ἔχει ἕνα δύσκολο χρῶμα ἀπὸ παλιὰ βήματα
    ποὺ μεῖναν στὴ μέση
ἀπὸ παλιὰ πιθάρια θαμμένα στὴν αὐλή, καὶ πάνω τους ἡ
    κούραση καὶ τὸ χορτάρι.

Δυὸ σκοτωμένοι, πέντε σκοτωμένοι, δώδεκα — πόσοι καὶ πόσοι.
Κάθε ὥρα ἔχει τὸ σκοτωμένο της. Πίσω ἀπ᾽ τὰ παράθυρα
στέκουν αὐτοὶ ποὺ λείπουν καὶ τὸ σταμνὶ μὲ τὸ νερὸ ποὺ δὲν
    ἤπιαν.

Κι αὐτὸ τὸ ἀστέρι ποὺ ἔπεσε στὴν ἄκρη τῆς βραδιᾶς
εἶναι σὰν τὸ κομμένο αὐτὶ ποὺ δὲν ἀκούει τὰ τριζόνια
ποὺ δὲν ἀκούει τὶς δικαιολογίες μας — δὲν καταδέχεται
ν᾽ ἀκούσει τὰ τραγούδια μας — μονάχο, μονάχο,
μονάχο, ἀποκομμένο, ἀδιάφορο γιὰ καταδίκη ἢ γιὰ δικαίωση.

The afternoon is all fallen plaster, black stones, dry thorns.
The afternoon has a difficult color made up of old footsteps halted
    in mid-stride,
of old jars buried in the courtyard, covered by fatigue and straw.

Two killed, five killed, twelve—so very many.
Each hour has its killing. Behind the windows
stand those who are missing, and the jug full of water they didn't
    drink.

And that star that fell at the edge of evening
is like the severed ear that doesn't hear the crickets,
doesn't hear our excuses—doesn't condescend
to hear our songs—alone, alone,
alone, cut off totally, indifferent to condemnation or vindication.

Κυριακή. Γυαλίζουν τὰ κουμπιὰ στὰ σακκάκια
σὰ μικρὰ γέλια. Τὸ λεωφορεῖο ἔφυγε.
Κάτι εὔθυμες φωνὲς — παράξενο
νὰ μπορεῖς ν' ἀκοῦς καὶ ν' ἀποκρίνεσαι. Κάτω ἀπ' τὰ πεῦκα
ἕνας ἐργάτης μαθαίνει φυσαρμόνικα. Μιὰ γυναίκα
εἶπε σὲ κάποιον καλημέρα — μιὰ τόσο ἁπλὴ καὶ φυσικὴ
    καλημέρα
ποὺ θἄθελες κ' ἐσὺ νὰ μάθεις φυσαρμόνικα κάτω ἀπ' τὰ πεῦκα.

Ὄχι διαίρεση ἢ ἀφαίρεση. Νὰ μπορεῖς νὰ κοιτάζεις
ἔξω ἀπὸ σένα — ζεστασιὰ καὶ ἡσυχία. Νὰ μὴν εἶσαι
«μονάχα ἐσύ», μὰ «καὶ ἐσύ». Μιὰ μικρὴ πρόσθεση,
μιὰ μικρὴ πράξη τῆς πρακτικῆς ἀριθμητικῆς, εὐκολονόητη,
ποὺ κ' ἕνα παιδὶ μπορεῖ νὰ τὴν πετύχει παίζοντας στὸ φῶς
    τὰ δάχτυλά του
ἢ παίζοντας αὐτὴ τὴ φυσαρμόνικα γιὰ ν' ἀκούσει ἡ γυναίκα.

Sunday. The buttons on jackets gleam
like scattered laughter. The bus left.
Some happy voices—strange
that you are able to listen and answer. Under the pine trees
a worker is learning how to play a mouth organ. A woman
said good morning to someone—such a simple and natural good
    morning
that you too would like to learn how to play a mouth organ under
    the pine trees.

No division or subtraction. To be able to look
outside yourself—warmth and peacefulness. Not to be
"only you" but "you too." A little addition,
a little practical arithmetic, easily grasped,
that even a child can manage to handle, playing his fingers against
    the light
or playing that mouth organ for the woman to hear.

Ἡ γυναίκα σηκώθηκε μπροστὰ στὸ τραπέζι. Τὰ λυπημένα
  της χέρια
κόβουν λεπτὲς φέτες λεμόνι γιὰ τὸ τσάι
σὰν κίτρινους τροχοὺς γιὰ ἕνα πολὺ μικρὸ ἁμαξάκι
παιδιάστικου παραμυθιοῦ. Ὁ νεαρὸς ἀξιωματικὸς ἀντίκρυ της
χωμένος στὴν παλιὰ πολυθρόνα. Δὲν τὴν κοιτάει.
Ἀνάβει τὸ τσιγάρο του. Τὸ χέρι του μὲ τὸ σπίρτο τρέμει
φωτίζοντας τὸ τρυφερὸ πηγούνι του καὶ τὸ χεράκι τοῦ
  φλιτζανιοῦ. Τὸ ρολόι
κρατάει μιὰ στιγμὴ τὸ καρδιοχτύπι του. Κάτι ἔχει ἀναβληθεῖ.
Ἡ στιγμὴ πέρασε. Εἶναι ἀργά. Νὰ πιοῦμε τὸ τσάι μας.
Μπορεῖ λοιπὸν νἄρθει ἕνας θάνατος μ᾽ ἕνα τέτοιο ἁμαξάκι;
Νὰ περάσει καὶ νὰ φύγει; Ν᾽ ἀπομείνει μονάχα
ἐτοῦτο τὸ ἁμαξάκι μὲ τὶς κίτρινες ροδίτσες τοῦ λεμονιοῦ
σταματημένο τόσα χρόνια σὲ μιὰ πάροδο μὲ σβηστοὺς
  φανοστάτες
κ᾽ ὕστερα ἕνα μικρὸ τραγούδι, λίγος ἀχνός, κ᾽ ὕστερα τίποτα;

The woman stood up in front of the table. Her sad hands
begin to cut thin slices of lemon for tea
like yellow wheels for a very small carriage
made for a child's fairy tale. The young officer sitting opposite
is buried in the old armchair. He doesn't look at her.
He lights up his cigarette. His hand holding the match trembles,
throwing light on his tender chin and the teacup's handle. The
   clock
holds its heartbeat for a moment. Something has been postponed.
The moment has gone. It's too late now. Let's drink our tea.
Is it possible, then, for death to come in that kind of carriage?
To pass by and go away? And only this carriage to remain,
with its little yellow wheels of lemon
parked for so many years on a side street with unlit lamps,
and then a small song, a little mist, and then nothing?

Εἶναι πολὺ μακρινὲς οἱ γυναῖκες. Τὰ σεντόνια τους μυρίζουν
καληνύχτα.
᾿Ακουμπᾶνε τὸ ψωμὶ στὸ τραπέζι γιὰ νὰ μὴ νιώσουμε πὼς
λείπουν.
Τότε καταλαβαίνουμε πὼς φταίξαμε. Σηκωνόμαστε ἀπ᾿ τὴν
καρέκλα καὶ λέμε:
«Κουράστηκες πολὺ σήμερα», ἢ «ἄσε, θ᾿ ἀνάψω ἐγὼ τὴ
λάμπα».

῞Οταν ἀνάβουμε τὸ σπίρτο, ἐκείνη στρέφει ἀργὰ πηγαίνοντας
μὲ μιὰν ἀνεξήγητη προσήλωση πρὸς τὴν κουζίνα. ῾Η πλάτη
της
εἶναι ἕνα πικραμένο βουναλάκι φορτωμένο μὲ πολλοὺς
νεκροὺς —
τοὺς νεκροὺς τῆς φαμίλιας, τοὺς δικούς της νεκροὺς καὶ τὸν
δικό σου.

᾿Ακοῦς τὸ βῆμα της νὰ τρίζει στὰ παλιὰ σανίδια
ἀκοῦς τὰ πιάτα νὰ κλαῖνε στὴν πιατοθήκη κ᾿ ὕστερα ἀκούγεται
τὸ τραῖνο ποὺ παίρνει τοὺς φαντάρους γιὰ τὸ μέτωπο.

Women are very distant. Their sheets smell of "good night."
They set the bread down on the table so that we don't feel they're
    absent.
Then we recognize that it was our fault. We get up out of the chair
    and say:
"You worked awfully hard today," or "Forget it, I'll light the lamp."

When we strike the match, she turns slowly and moves off
with inexplicable concentration toward the kitchen. Her back
is a bitterly sad hill loaded with many dead—
the family's dead, her dead, your own death.

You hear her footsteps creak on the old floorboards,
hear the dishes cry in the rack, and then you hear
the train that's taking the soldiers to the front.

1. Ώσπου βράδιασε

Κρατούσε στὸ χέρι του τὸ χέρι της. Δὲ μιλοῦσε.
Ἄκουγε πέρα, ἴσως καὶ μέσα του,
τὸν ἄφθονο σφυγμὸ τῆς θάλασσας.
Ἡ θάλασσα, τὰ πεῦκα, οἱ λόφοι, εἶταν τὸ χέρι της.
Ἄν δὲν τῆς τόλεγε, πῶς θὰ κρατοῦσε τὸ χέρι της;

Σώπαιναν, ὥσπου βράδιασε. Κάτω ἀπ᾽ τὰ δέντρα,
εἶταν μονάχα ἕνα ἄγαλμα μὲ τὰ δυὸ χέρια του κομμένα.

2. Μιὰ γυναίκα

Ἡ νύχτα αὐτή, ἀπρυσπέλαστη, κανέναν δὲ φιλάει —
μόνη μέσα στὸ φόβο της μὴ δὲ βρεθεῖ κανεὶς νὰ τὴ φιλήσει.

Μὲ πέντε ἀστέρια - δάχτυλα κρύβει μιὰ τούφα ἄσπρα μαλλιά
κ᾽ εἶναι ἔτσι ὡραία σὰν ἄρνηση τοῦ πιὸ ὡραίου ἑαυτοῦ της.

3. Τί φταῖμε;

Κάτω ἀπ᾽ τὴ γλώσσα σου εἶναι τὰ λεπτὰ κλωνάκια τοῦ
    ἄνηθου,
οἱ σπόροι τῶν σταφυλιῶν καὶ οἱ ἶνες τῶν ροδάκινων.
Μέσα στὴ σκιὰ ποὺ ρίχνουν τὰ ματόκλαδά σου
εἶναι μιὰ γῆ ζεστή. Μπορῶ νὰ ξαπλώσω
καὶ νὰ ξεκουραστῶ ἀνερώτητα, εἶπε.

Τί θέλει λοιπὸν αὐτὸ τό «πιὸ πέρα»;
Καὶ σὺ τί φταῖς, ἀνυποψίαστη, νὰ μένεις μὲ τὰ φύλλα;
Ὡραία κι ἁπλὴ μὲς στὸ χρυσὸ σχῆμα τῆς ζέστας σου;
Κ᾽ ἐγὼ τί φταίω νὰ προχωρῶ μέσα στὴ νύχτα
δέσμιος στὴν ἐλευθερία μου, εἶπε, τιμωρώντας ὁ τιμωρημένος;

1. Until it turned dark

He held her hand in his. He didn't speak.
He heard farther off, and maybe inside him,
the abundant pulse of the sea.
The sea, the pine trees, the hills were her hand.
If he didn't tell her so, how could he hold her hand?

They were still, until it turned dark. Under the trees
there was only a statue with both hands broken off.

2. A Woman

That night: unapproachable, she kisses nobody—
alone in her fear that no one will be found to kiss her.

With five star-fingers she hides a tuft of white hair,
and she is so beautiful as the denial of her most beautiful self.

3. Why is it our fault?

Under your tongue are the delicate sprigs of brill,
seeds from grapes and peach fibers.
In the shade cast by your eyelashes
there is warm country. I can lie down
and rest myself unquestioning, he said.

Now what does it mean, this "farther ahead"?
Why is it your fault, unsuspecting, for staying among the leaves—
beautiful, simple, in the golden shape of your heat?
And why is it my fault for going ahead in the night,
captive in my freedom, he said, the punished one punishing?

Φτωχειὰ μουσικὴ τὸ Σαββατόβραδο, ποὺ βγαίνει ἀπ᾽ τὸ
   χοροδιδασκαλεῖο τῆς συνοικίας,
φτωχειὰ μουσικὴ, ξεπαγιασμένη, μὲ τὰ ξυλοπάπουτσα,—
κάθε ποὺ ἀνοίγει ἡ ἄβαφτη πόρτα πετάγεται στὸ δρόμο,
τουρτουρίζει κάτω ἀπ᾽ τὸ φανάρι της γωνιᾶς,
ρίχνει μιὰ ματιὰ σ᾽ ἕνα ψηλὸ παράθυρο ἢ στὴ νύχτα,
ὕστερα χαμηλώνει τὰ μάτια στὴ λάσπη,
κάτι ψάχνει, κάτι περιμένει,
σὰν κάποιος νᾶναι ἄρρωστος κι ἀργεῖ ὁ γιατρός.

Φτωχειὰ μουσική. Κάνει κρύο. Κανέας δὲν ἀνοίγει τὸ παράθυρο
νὰ σὲ φιλέψει λίγο φῶς τῆς λάμπας, λίγη μαύρη σταφίδα,
νὰ σοῦ πεῖ θυμᾶμαι — πρὶν εἴκοσι - τριάντα χρόνια,
κάτι ἤχους ἀπὸ παλιὰ ἁμάξια στὴ βροχή,
ἕνα τοπίο θολὸ ζωγραφισμένο στὰ γυαλιὰ τοῦ Τέλλου Ἄγρα.

Μὰ τὰ παπούτσια εἶναι τρύπια, λασπωμένα·
τὰ ζευγαράκια βιάζονται στὸ δρόμο· δὲν ἀκοῦνε.
Ἕνας σταμάτησε σύρριζα στὸν τοῖχο. Δὲ σ᾽ ἀκούει, ὄχι.
Κάτι τοιχοκολλάει. Μονάχα τὸ μαχαίρι
ἐπάνω στὸ τραπέζι εἶναι μιὰ σκέψη καὶ μιὰ λάμψη.

Φτωχειὰ μουσική, ἂν χωρᾶς
ἔμπα ἀπ᾽ τὸν τρύπιο ἀγκώνα τῆς συνοικίας.

Poor Saturday night music coming from the neighborhood
   dancing school,
poor music, frozen, with wooden shoes—
every time the unpainted door opens the music rushes out into the
   street,
shivers under the light on the corner,
glances at a high window or at the night,
then lowers its look to the mud,
searching for something, waiting for something,
as though somebody's sick and the doctor's slow in coming.

Poor music. It's cold. Nobody opens a window
to treat you to a bit of lamplight, some black raisins,
to tell you: I remember—twenty or thirty years ago—
certain sounds from old carriages in the rain,
a blurred landscape painted on the glasses of Tellos Agras.*

But the shoes are full of holes and muddy;
the couples hurry down the street; they don't listen.
A man stops up against the wall. No, he doesn't hear you.
He glues something to the wall. Only the knife
on the table is a thought, a flash of light.

Poor music; if you can fit,
come in through the hole in the neighborhood's elbow.

* Tellos Agras is the pseudonym of Evangelos Ioannou (1899-1944), the poet and
critic. From 1923 to 1940 he wrote poems ranging from the bucolic mode to the late
Symbolist mode, the latter under the influence of Moréas and Laforgue. Ritsos has
remarked in conversation that he remembers Tellos Agras in particular for his focus
on themes from "the everyday life of neighborhoods."

Μουσκεμένες οἱ στέγες γυαλίζουν στὸ φεγγαρόφωτο. Οἱ
   γυναῖκες
τυλίγονται στὸ μποξά τους. Βιάζονται νὰ κρυφτοῦν στὸ σπίτι
   τους.
Ἄν μείνουν λίγο ἀκόμη στὸ κατώφλι, θὰ τὶς δεῖ τὸ φεγγάρι νὰ
   κλαῖνε.

Αὐτὸς ὑποψιάζεται μέσα σὲ κάθε καθρέφτη
μιὰν ἄλλη, διάφανη γυναίκα, ἀποκλεισμένη μὲς στὴ γύμνια
   της
— ὅσο κι ἂν θέλεις νὰ τὴν ξυπνήσεις, δὲν ξυπνάει.
Ἀποκοιμήθηκε μυρίζοντας ἕνα ἄστρο.

Κι αὐτὸς μυρίζει τὸ ἴδιο ἐκεῖνο ἀστέρι ξαγρυπνώντας.

Drenched, the roofs glisten in the moon's light. The women
wrap themselves in their shawls. They rush to hide in their houses.
If they hover a little longer on the threshold, the moon will catch
   them crying.

That man suspects that in every mirror
there's another, transparent woman, locked in her nakedness
—much as you may want to wake her, she won't wake up.
She fell asleep smelling a star.

And he lies awake smelling that same star.

Αὐτὸ τὸ παράθυρο εἶναι μονάχο.
Αὐτὸ τὸ ἀστέρι εἶναι μονάχο,
σὰν ἕνα τσιγάρο ξεχασμένο στὸ τραπέζι —
καπνίζει, καπνίζει στὸ γαλάζιο, μονάχο.

Κ' ἐγὼ εἶμαι μονάχος, εἶπε.
'Ανάβω τὸ τσιγάρο μου, καπνίζω.
Καπνίζω καὶ σκέφτομαι. Δὲν εἶμαι μονάχος.

This window is alone.
This star is alone,
like a cigarette forgotten on the table—
smoking, smoking in the blue, alone.

And I'm alone, he said.
I light my cigarette, I smoke.
I smoke and meditate. I'm not alone.

Νυχτώνει ἀργὰ στὴ συνοικία. Δὲ μᾶς παίρνει ὁ ὕπνος.
Περιμένουμε νὰ ξημερώσει. Περιμένουμε
νὰ χτυπήσει ἡ ἥλιος σὰ σφυρὶ τὶς λαμαρίνες τῶν ὑπόστεγων,
νὰ χτυπήσει τὸ μέτωπό μας, τὴν καρδιά μας,
νὰ γίνει ἕνας ἦχος ν᾽ ἀκουστεῖ ὁ ἦχος — ἕνας ἦχος ἄλλος,
γιατὶ ἡ σιωπὴ εἶναι γεμάτη πυροβολισμοὺς ἀπὸ ἄγνωστα
    σημεῖα.

It turns dark slowly in the neighborhood. We can't sleep.
We wait for daybreak. We wait
for the sun to strike the tin of the sheds like a hammer,
to strike our foreheads, our hearts,
to become a sound, for the sound to be heard—a different sound,
because the silence is full of gun shots from unknown places.

Τὸν εἴδαμε γονατισμένον στὴν πιὸ ὄρθια στάση, νὰ φυσάει
    μὲ τὴν ἀνάσα του
κάτω ἀπ' τὸ μεγάλο καζάνι, νὰ συντηρεῖ τὴ φωτιὰ
καταναλίσκοντας τὴ φωτιά του. Ἀνυπόμονος — λαχάνιαζε
πιεσμένος ἀπ' τὸ δέρμα του, μὴ χωρώντας μέσα στὸ δέρμα
    του.

Τὸ φῶς ἔτρεμε πέρα στὸν ὁρίζοντα καθὼς ἀνοιγοκλεῖναν τὰ
    πλευρά του.
Ὁ σφυγμός του φούσκωνε τὶς ρῶγες τῶν σταφυλιῶν
κ' ἔκανε τὰ καινούργια φύλλα νὰ στροβιλίζονται ἀσάλευτα.

Ἔτσι, σκυμμένος, ξοδεύτηκε γιὰ νὰ μείνουμε ὄρθιοι,
ἐσὺ κ' ἐγώ, χωρὶς ποτέ του νὰ σκεφτεῖ
πὼς θἄπρεπε μιὰ μέρα νὰ τοῦ χρωστᾶμε κάτι.

Μπορεῖς, λοιπόν, νὰ μὴ μείνεις τουλάχιστον ὄρθιος;

We saw him kneeling in the most upright posture, blowing his
     breath
under the huge copper pot in order to feed the fire
by consuming his own fire. Impatient, breathing hard,
constrained by his skin, unable to fit inside his skin.

The light trembled at the horizon as his ribs opened and closed.
His pulse swelled the skins of grapes
and made the new leaves whirl motionless.

So, bent over, he spent himself so that we could remain standing
     upright,
you and me, without his once considering
that we should one day owe him something.

How then can you not remain upright at least?

Ἐσὺ δὲ θὰ μοῦ πεῖς εὐχαριστῶ,
ὅπως δὲ λὲς εὐχαριστῶ στοὺς χτύπους τῆς καρδιᾶς σου
ποὺ σμιλεύουν τὸ πρόσωπο τῆς ζωῆς σου.

Ὅμως ἐγὼ θὰ σοῦ λέω εὐχαριστῶ
γιατὶ γνωρίζω τί σοῦ ὀφείλω.

Αὐτὸ τὸ εὐχαριστῶ εἶναι τὸ τραγούδι μου.

You won't say thanks to me
just as you don't say thanks to your heartbeats
carving out the face of your life.

But I will say thanks to you
because I know what I owe you.

That thanks is my song.

Parentheses, 1950-61

Άσε γιά μιά στιγμή νά κλείσουμε τά μάτια
ν'ἀκούσουμε τή μητέρα νά πλένει τά πιάτα στήν κουζίνα
ν'ἀκούσουμε νά πέφτουν στό συρτάρι τά μαχαιροπίρουνα
ν'ἀκούσουμε στό διάδρομο τό θρόϊσμα τοῦ φουστανιοῦ της
καί τό χαμόγελο τῆς Παναγίας νά σεργιανάει στό εἰκονοστάσι.

Αὔριο δέ θἄμαστε ἄρρωστοι. Κοίταξε τό θερμόμετρο.
Εἶναι ἀκόμη ζεστό ἀπ' τή μασκάλη μας.
Πάτερ ἡμῶν ὁ ἐν τοῖς οὐρανοῖς
πές στή μικρή ἐξαδέλφη μας νἄρθει αὔριο
νά βγοῦμε ἕνα μικρό περίπατο στό δάσος μέ τά ἐλάφια.

Θά τῆς μαζέψω φρέσκα μύγδαλα.
Ἕνα γαλάζιο ἐλάφι θἄρθει
πάτερ ἡμῶν ὥστε νά κοιμηθοῦμε
ἕνα γαλά - γαλάζιο ἐλάφι
πάτερ ἡμῶν
ὁ ἐν τοῖς
οὐρανοῖς.

Let us close our eyes a moment
so that we can hear the mother washing dishes in the kitchen
so that we can hear the knives and forks falling into the drawer
so that we can hear the rustle of her dress in the corridor
and the Holy Virgin's smile wandering in the iconostasis.

Tomorrow we won't be sick any longer. Look at the thermometer.
It's still warm from our armpit.
Our father who art in heaven
tell our little cousin to come tomorrow
so that we can take a short walk in the forest with the deer.

I will gather fresh almonds for her.
A blue deer will come,
our father, so that we can sleep
a blue blue deer
our father
who art
in heaven.

Πάντα ἀργοπορημένοι. Φταίει καί τό ρολόϊ μας — πάει πίσω.
Ψάχνουμε γιά τή θέση μας στά σκοτεινά, ὅπως τότε
στήν πλατεία τοῦ θεάτρου — εἶχε ἀρχίσει ἡ παράσταση
    ἀπ' ὥρα —
σκοντάφτοντας στά γόνατα τῶν θεατῶν καί σέ ξύλινες πλάτες.
Κι ἄξαφνα ἀνάψανε τά φῶτα μές στά χειροκροτήματα. Κ'ἐμεῖς
ὄρθιοι νά ψάχνουμε ἀκόμη σάμπως νά χειροκροτοῦσαν
ἐμᾶς πού δέν τ'ἀξίζαμε. Φιαχτήκαμε στό πρῶτο κάθισμα
πατώντας τά πόδια μιᾶς ἄσκημης γριᾶς. Αὐτή δέ φώναξε.

We're always late. Our watch is at fault too—it's slow.
We search for our seat in the dark, like that time
in the pit of the theatre—the show had long since started—
stumbling over knees in the aisles and over wooden backrests.
And suddenly they turned on the lights during the clapping. And
    we
standing up, still searching, as though they were clapping for us
who didn't deserve it. We settled in the first seat
stepping on the feet of an ugly old woman. She didn't yell.

Ξοδεύαμε βλέμματα, λόγια, κινήσεις.
Τά μεσημέρια κοιτούσαμε κατά τή θάλασσα κάπως ἀμήχανοι
ἀνάμεσα ἀπ'τίς φωνές τῶν τζιτζικιῶν κι ἀπ'τά φύλλα—
σκόρπιες ματιές γιά νά μή δοῦμε ὅ, τι εἴδαμε κιόλας.
Τό βράδι ὁ ἴσκιος ἔκρυβε τούς ξέχωρους ἴσκιους μας.
Ἕνας στενόμακρος ξύλινος πάγκος
μέ ἀπούλητες ἀθλητικές φανέλες
ἔστεκε ἀπόμερα στήν πλατεία τῆς συνοικίας.
Ἡ νύχτα μύριζε σβησμένο κερί.
Ἄλλο πρόσχημα πιά δέ μᾶς ἔμενε παρά ν'ἀκοῦμε
τό λόξυγκα ἑνός ἄστρου πίσω ἀπ'τήν πόρτα.

We spent glances, words, movement.
At noon we would gaze toward the sea somehow at a loss
among the sounds of cicadas, among the leaves—
scattered looks so that we wouldn't see what we'd already seen.
In the evening the shade hid our separate shadows.
A long, narrow wooden bench
with unsold shirts for athletes
stood out of the way in the neighborhood square.
The night smelled of extinguished candles.
No other pretense was left to us but that of listening
to the hiccup of a star behind the door.

Ὅ,τι κρατᾶς στά χέρια σου
τόσο προσεχτικά, μέ τόση ἀγάπη,
τόσο δικό σου, σύντροφε,
πρέπει νά τό χαρίσεις
γιά νά γίνει δικό σου.

Whatever you hold in your hands
so carefully, with so much love,
yours so totally, my companion,
you must give away
in order for it to become yours.

Εἶταν καλή ἡ γιαγιά, εἶταν ἥσυχη. Δίπλα στά μάτια της
εἶχε πολλές λιανές ρυτίδες σάν τά πετσετάκια τοῦ τσαγιοῦ
προσεχτικά κεντημένες. Εἶχε καί μιά ἀλαφριά καρδιά
σά μιά μικρή σακκούλα γεμάτη μπαμπάκι.

Ἔφυγε ἡ γιαγιά. Μπορεῖ νά πῆγε νά γνέσει τό μπαμπάκι της
στό παραγώνι τῆς μεγάλης νύχτας. Μά πῶς ἔγινε
νά βγεῖ ἡ γιαγιά ἀπ᾽ τό σπίτι, καί νά βρέχει κιόλας
καί νά μήν ἔχει πάρει οὔτε τό μάλλινο σάλι της.

Κλαίει ἡ μικρή ὑπηρέτρια στήν καρέκλα τοῦ διαδρόμου.
Κλαίει κ᾽ἡ μικρή βροχή στά σκαλοπάτια τοῦ Ἑλκόμενου.
Τό μικρότερο ἐγγόνι δέν ἔκλαιγε, βλέποντας τί ὄμορφα πού
    κλαῖνε
ἡ βροχή, τά σκαλοπάτια, ἡ καρέκλα κ᾽ἡ μικρή ὑπηρέτρια
γιά τή μικρή γιαγιά πού γνέθει τώρα ἀθώρητη τό μαλακό
    μπαμπάκι της.

The grandmother was a good woman, she was quiet. Beside her
  eyes
there were many thin wrinkles like those of tea napkins
carefully embroidered. She also had a light heart
like a small bag full of cotton.

The grandmother left. Maybe she went to spin her cotton
on the edge of the great night's fireplace. But how is it possible
that the grandmother went out of the house, and in the rain,
and without taking her woolen shawl even?

The little maid is crying on a chair in the hallway.
The light rain is also crying on the steps of Elkomenos Church.*
The smallest grandchild didn't cry, seeing how beautifully
the rain, the steps, the chair, and the little maid all were crying
over the little grandmother who now spins her wool unseen.

*The allusion is to a church in Monemvasia (Laconia), the town where the poet
spent his childhood. Among the icons in the church is one depicting Christ standing
with hands bound by a rope. *Elkomenos* means "The Dragged One."

Καθόταν μόνος στό σκοτάδι τῆς κάμαρας καπνίζοντας.
Τίποτα δέ φαινόταν. Μόνο ἡ λάμψη τοῦ τσιγάρου του
μετακινιόταν πότε-πότε ἀργά, προσεχτικά
κ᾽εἴτανε σά νά τάϊζε μ᾽ἕνα ἀσημένιο κουταλάκι
ἕνα ἄρρωστο κορίτσι, ἤ σά νά περιποιόταν
μ᾽ἕνα μικρό νυστέρι τό τραῦμα ἑνός ἄστρου.

He sat alone in the darkness of the room smoking.
Nothing was visible. Only the glow of his cigarette
moved slowly now and then, carefully,
as though he were feeding a sick girl
with a silver spoon, or as though he were treating
some star's wound with a small lancet.

Πολλές φορές τά χέρια εἶναι σάν πρόσωπα
ἤ σάν ὁλόκληρα σώματα. Τοῦτα τά χέρια
στέκονται ἀνόρεξα στήν πρώϊμη ἄνοιξη,
φτερνίζονται, βήχουν, γκρινιάζουν, σωπαίνουν,
ὅπως δυό γέροι στό σκαμνί τους, ξεκούμπωτοι,
μέ τά γεννητικά τους ὄργανα μαραμένα στόν ἥλιο.

Ἀντίκρυ, μιά γυναίκα θηλάζει τό βρέφος της.
Τά χέρια της, παρ' ὅτι ἀσάλευτα, εἶναι
δυό ὁλόγυμνοι δρομεῖς σ'ἕνα μεγάλο μαρμάρινο στίβο.

Often hands are like faces
or like whole bodies. These hands
remain listless in the premature spring,
they sneeze, cough, complain, grow silent,
like two old men on their stools, unbuttoned,
with their genitals withered in the sun.

Opposite, a woman suckles her infant.
Her hands, though motionless, are
two naked runners in a large marble arena.

Μῆνες καί μῆνες, βδομάδες, ἡμέρες—ἀμάθητος χρόνος.
Ὁ Ἀπρίλης μέ μυωπικά γυαλιά στό παγκάκι τοῦ κήπου.
Ὁ Ἰούλιος σοῦ ἀπαγορεύει νά κοιμηθεῖς μονάχος.
Ὁ Σεπτέμβρης θυμᾶται τά κλειδωμένα σπίτια—
δυό χάρτινα λουλούδια καί μιά μαύρη τσατσάρα στό τραπέζι.
Τόν Νοέμβρη ἕνας ἄνθρωπος κρατάει μιά πέτρα στό γόνατό
    του.
Γενάρης, Φλεβάρης,—λείπουν ὅλοι στά ξένα.
Ἀπελπισμένες χειρονομίες τοῦ ἀνέμου
μπροστά στήν τζαμόπορτα τοῦ κλειστοῦ ξενοδοχείου.
Ὕστερα ἡ σιωπηλή παραδουλεύτρα βγαίνει τά χαράματα
μ᾽ ἕνα μεγάλο σφουγγάρι νά καθαρίσει τά τζάμια.

Months on months, weeks, days—unlearnable year.
April with myopic glasses on the garden bench.
July forbids you to sleep alone.
September remembers the locked houses—
two paper flowers and a black large-toothed comb on the table.
In November some man holds a stone on his knee.
January, February—everyone has gone abroad.
Desperate gestures by the wind
in front of the closed hotel's glass door.
Then the silent charwoman emerges at dawn
with a large sponge to clean the windows.

Ἡ *νύχτα σέ γδύνει*. Τά χέρια της τρέμουν.
Ὁλόγυμνο τό σῶμα σου λάμπει στούς ἴσκιους.

Ἐκεῖνο τό σοφό μηδέν πούσφιγγε τό λαιμό μας
κόβεται ξαφνικά στά δυό
σάν τό βρασμένο αὐγό μέ τό μαχαίρι.

Night undresses you. Her hands tremble.
All naked, your body shines in the shadows.

That wise zero that squeezed our necks
is suddenly cut in two
like a boiled egg sliced by a knife.

Βαθειά βοή στροβιλιζότανε γύρω ἀπό κάθε ἀστέρι.
Μιά δύναμη θλιμμένη μυστική
ἔκανε σκοτεινά τά δέντρα.

Μόνο σημεῖο προσανατολισμοῦ μές στό σκοτάδι
δυό ἐλάχιστοι κύκλοι ἀπό φῶς—
τά γόνατα τῆς σιωπηλῆς γυναίκας.

Deep roaring whirled around every star.
Some power, secret, grieving,
made the trees dark.

The only point of orientation in the dark:
two minute circles of light,
the knees of the silent woman.

Δέ θέλω τίποτα—έλεγε. Εἶναι ἥσυχα ἔτσι.
Σ' ὅλο τό μάκρος τοῦ φθινόπωρου φαίνονται
τά κλειστά τζάμια τοῦ γηροκομείου.

Ἐκεῖνο τό σκοινί πού δέναν τό ἄλογο
μένει μονάχο τώρα γύρω στόν κορμό τοῦ δέντρου.

I don't want anything, he said. It's quiet like this.
Visible the whole length of autumn
are the closed windows of the old-people's home.

That rope they used for tying up the horse
now lies alone around the tree's trunk.

Ἐκεῖνα πού καιρό λογάριαζαν δέ βγῆκαν.
Κατέβασαν τίς σημαῖες ἀπ' τά μπαλκόνια.
Οἱ τοῖχοι μυρίζουν πολλή ξενιτειά. Τώρα
τό μόνο στήριγμα εἶναι ἡ ἔλλειψη κάθε δικαιολογίας.

That which they'd anticipated for some time didn't happen.
On the balconies they took the flags down.
The walls smell strongly of unfamiliarity. Now
the only prop is the lack of any excuse.

Τό βράδι στεκόταν ἀντίκρυ μας ὅμοιο μέ τήν πρόσοψη
ἑνός διόροφου ὀρφανοτροφείου μέ κλειστά παράθυρα.

Τήν ἄλλη μέρα, μιά γυναίκα, κάτω ἀπ᾽τά δέντρα,
ἔβγαζε ἕνα ἀγκάθι ἀπ᾽τό πέλμα της —

τό ἴδιο ἐκεῖνο ἀγκάθι πού πατᾶμε κάθε νύχτα.

The night stood opposite us just like the façade
of a two-story orphanage with closed windows.

The next day, a woman, under the trees,
took a thorn out of the sole of her foot—

that same thorn which we step on every night.

Ὁ κόσμος εἶναι μιά μακριά σειρά τραγούδια
πού πρέπει νά τά τραγουδήσεις — εἶπε.
Ὁ κόσμος εἶναι ἕνα δέντρο ὅλο καρπούς
πού μόνο τό σπαθί τούς κόβει.

Τό σπαθί κόβει τό τραγούδι. Τό τραγούδι
στομώνει τό σπαθί. Τί νά διαλέξεις ; — εἶπε.
Πῶς νά διαλέξεις μές στά διαλεγμένα κιόλας ;
Ὁ κόσμος εἶναι ἕνα βαθύ κλειστό τραγούδι.

The world is a long cycle of songs
that you should sing, he said.
The world is a tree full of fruit
that only a sword can cut.

The sword cuts the song. The song
blunts the sword. What can you choose? he said.
How can you choose between the already chosen?
The world is a deep closed song.

Κινοῦσε τά μεγάλα δάχτυλά του στό τραπέζι
σά νά τἄχωνε μέσα στό ποτάμι. Δέ μιλοῦσε.
Τό πρόσωπό του εἶταν χυμένο στό σίδερο.
Ἔνιωθες τό χλιμίντρισμα ἑνός κόκκινου ἀλόγου
στριφωμένο στίς ραφές τοῦ σακκακιοῦ του.
Αὐτός δέ χόρευε. Ἔρριχνε στούς βιολιτζῆδες
μεγάλα, δυνατά νομίσματα γιά νά χορεύουν οἱ ἄλλοι.

He moved his large fingers on the table
as though thrusting them into the river. He didn't speak.
His face was cast in iron.
You sensed the whinnying of a red horse
hemmed inside the seams of his jacket.
He didn't dance. He threw large, robust coins
to the violinists so that others would dance.

Βραδιάζει. Οἱ φτωχογυναικοῦλες περιμένουν ἀκόμη
οὐρά μπροστά στό φοῦρνο. Οἱ ποιητές περιμένουν
οὐρά μπροστά στό νέο φεγγάρι, παρ᾽ὅτι
καί τό ἐλάχιστο χόρτο στήν ἄκρη τοῦ δρόμου
δέν ἐπιτρέπει καθόλου τή ματαιότητα.

Ἕνα λεωφορεῖο πέρασε. Ἀνάβουν τά φῶτα.
Τί ἁπλᾶ πού θά μιλούσαμε ἀπόψε.

It turns dark. The poor women are still waiting in line
in front of the bakery. The poets are waiting in line
in front of the new moon, even though
the sparest grass at the edge of the road
permits no futility at all.

A bus went by. The lights come on.
How simply we would have talked tonight.

Νύχτα. Δέν ἀκουγόταν τίποτα. Μόνο ἡ βοή τῆς ἀπόστασης κ᾽ἐκείνη ἡ διάφανη ἀκαθόριστη σελήνη, πού τό φῶς της ἔμενε ἀκόμη ἀμορφοποίητο καί τήν πονοῦσε.

Night. No sound at all. Only the roaring of space
and that transparent undefined moon whose light
remained still unformed and hurt her.

Κάποτε, μέσα σ'ὅλο τό δάσος ἕνα δέντρο μονάχα
σείεται σύφυλλο, χωρίς καθόλου νά φυσήσει ἀέρας. Κι
    ἀμέσως
μαρμαρώνει ξανά σά σβηστός πολυέλαιος
στό κέντρο τῆς νύχτας, κάνοντας πιό γρήγορες
τίς ἀναπνοές τῶν βοσκῶν, τῶν ἀλόγων, τῶν ἄστρων.

Sometimes in the whole forest there is only one tree
all of whose leaves stir, without any breeze at all. And right away
it turns marble-still again like an unlit chandelier
in the night's center, quickening
the breathing of shepherds, horses, stars.

Ὁ φύλακας τοῦ Μουσείου κάπνιζε μπροστά στή μάντρα.
Τά πρόβατα βόσκαν ἀνάμεσα στά μάρμαρα.
Πιό κάτου πλέναν οἱ γυναῖκες στό ποτάμι.
᾽Ακούγονταν ὁ χτύπος τοῦ σφυριοῦ στό σιδεράδικο.
Ὁ βοσκός σφύριξε. Τά πρόβατα τρέξαν κοντά του
σά νά τρέξαν τά μάρμαρα. Ὁ χοντρός σβέρκος τοῦ νεροῦ
ἔλαμπε ὁλόδροσος πίσω ἀπ᾽ τίς πικροδάφνες. Μιά γυναίκα
ἅπλωνε τά πλυμένα ροῦχα στούς θάμνους καί στ᾽ ἀγάλματα —
τό σώβρακο τοῦ ἄντρα της τό ἅπλωσε στούς ὤμους τῆς Ἥρας.

Ξένη, γαλήνια, σιωπηλή οἰκειότητα — χρόνια καί χρόνια.
    Κάτω στ᾽ ἀκρογιάλι
περνοῦσαν οἱ ψαράδες μέ πανέρια στό κεφάλι τους
γεμάτα ψάρια, σάν νά κουβαλοῦσαν στενόμακρες λάμψεις
χρυσές, τριανταφυλλιές, μενεξεδένιες, — ἡ ἴδια ἐκείνη πομπή
    μεταφέροντας
τό μακρύ, πολυκέντητο πέπλο τῆς θεᾶς, πού τίς προάλλες τό
    κόψαμε
νά σιάξουμε κουρτίνες καί τραπεζομάντηλα γιά τά σπίτια μας
    πού ἄδειασαν.

The museum guard was smoking in front of the sheepfold.
The sheep were grazing among the marble ruins.
Farther down the women were washing in the river.
You could hear the beat of the hammer in the blacksmith's shop.
The shepherd whistled. The sheep ran to him
as though the marble ruins were running. The water's thick nape
shone with coolness behind the oleanders. A woman
spread her washed clothing on the shrubs and the statues—
she spread her husband's underpants on Hera's shoulders.

Foreign, peaceful, silent intimacy—years on years. Down on the
    shore
the fishermen passed by with broad baskets full of fish
on their heads, as though they were carrying long and narrow
    flashes of light:
gold, rose, and violet—the same as that procession bearing
the long, richly embroidered veil of the goddess that we cut up the
    other day
to arrange as curtains and tablecloths in our emptied houses.

Ὅλη ἡ πλαγιά στρωμένη κουκουνάρια καί πευκοβελόνες.
Στήν κορυφὴ σταθήκαμε ν᾽ἀφουγκραστοῦμε κάτω.
Ἡ ρεματιά μέ τά πλατάνια βούϊζε ἀπόμακρη
μ᾽ἄγριους κρωγμούς πουλιῶν καί ποταμιῶν. ᾽Αραιό τιτίβισμα
δεητικό, ἑνός κότσυφα, ψιχάλιζε
τήν παγωμένη ἑσπέρα, πάνω ἀπ᾽τό μεγάλο θόρυβο.

᾽Εδῶ ζευγάρωσαν τ᾽ἀγέρωχα ἄλογα
ἀδέσμευτα ἀπ᾽τόν ἔρωτα καί τήν πατρότητα. ῾Ο ὁρίζοντας
εἶναι ἕνα ἀπέραντο χρεμέτισμα. ᾽Εδῶ πάνω
κανένα γονάτισμα δέ βρίσκει συχώρεση.

᾽Αμείλικτη ἡ ψυχή τοῦ βουνοῦ ἐπιτηροῦσε
πάνω ἀπ᾽τή γνώση καί τήν ἄγνοια τοῦ θανάτου, πανύψηλη
ἀπό τήν περηφάνεια τοῦ ἄσκοπου, τοῦ ἀπέραντα παρόντος.

᾽Επάνω στ᾽ἄδεια μας παγούρια, ἀκούσαμε,
σάν πάνω σ᾽ἔνδοξα ταμποῦρλα, νά χτυποῦν
τά δάχτυλα τοῦ τρισμεγάλου ψύχους.

Σάμος — Λέκκα, 7.1.58

The whole slope of the hill spread with pine cones and pine
   needles.
At the top we stopped to listen downhill.
The ravine with the plane-trees roared in the distance
with the wild cawing of birds and rivers. The sparse chirping
plea of a blackbird sprinkled
the frozen evening above the great roar.

Here the arrogant horses coupled,
not bound by love and fatherhood. The horizon
is a limitless neighing. Up here
kneeling down finds no forgiveness.

Inexorably the soul of the mountain kept watch
over the knowledge and the ignorance of death, towering
with the pride of the aimless, of the boundless present.

Above our empty canteens we heard,
as above glorious drums,
the striking fingers of prodigious cold.

Samos—Lekka, 7.1.58

Κοιτοῦσε ἀπ' τά τζάμια τό πρωϊνό. Αἰσθανόταν μέ ἀκρίβεια
πῶς κυλάει τό γαλάζιο στό δέρμα τοῦ πουλιοῦ ἤ τοῦ σύννεφου.
Ὑποψιαζόταν πώς τήν ἴδια ἀφή διαθέτει καί τό δέντρο.
Ἀπό τούς καπνοδόχους ἔβγαινε ὁ καπνός σά νά ἐκμυστη-
    ρευόταν
τή ζεστασιά τῶν κλεισμένων ἀκόμη δωματίων.

Ἔτσι, κάθε πρωϊνό, ὅλα τά σπίτια καπνίζουν.
Κ' οἱ ἄντρες, πού βγαίνουν νωρίς γιά τή δουλειά τους,
ἀπ' τό κατώφλι κιόλας ἀνάβουν τό τσιγάρο τους, σά νά
    θυμιάζουν
κάποια ἄγνωστη ἀπλησίαστη θεότητα, ἐντελῶς δική τους.

He gazed at the morning through the windowpanes. He felt with
   precision
that the blue rolls along the bird's skin or the cloud's.
He suspected that the same sense of touch was at the tree's disposal
   also.
The smoke emerged from the chimneys as though confessing the
   secret
of heat in the rooms that were still closed.

In this way, every morning, all the houses smoke.
And the men, emerging early for work,
light up their cigarettes while still on the threshold, as though
   remembering
some unknown, unapproachable deity entirely their own.

Οἱ *νύχτες περνοῦσαν πολύ σκοτεινές.*
Μεγάλες φωνές τρέχαν στόν ἄνεμο.
Τήν ἄλλη μέρα δέ θυμόμαστε τίποτα.
Μιά βαθειά τρύπα εἶχε μείνει στό χρόνο.

Ἐκεῖ πού κούρνιαζε ὁ λύκος, ἀπόμεινε
μιά γούβα στρωμένη μέ ζεστές λυκότριχες.
Τώρα μποροῦσε νά πλαγιάσει ἐκεῖ ἕνα πρόβατο.

The nights passed very darkly.
Great cries ran in the wind.
The next day we didn't remember a thing.
There was a deep hole left in time.

There where the wolf had nestled in,
a pothole remained, spread with warm wolf-hair.
Now a sheep could lie down there.

Ἐφημερίδες, ἐξεγέρσεις, διαψεύσεις, ἀνακαλύψεις, γάμοι,
   θάνατοι·
ἱδρώτας, σκόνη, σκοτάδι, διανυκτερεῦον φαρμακεῖο·
μιά σκάλα ἀνεβαίνει στά τυφλά· κλοπές, ἐγκλήματα, ἀδικία·
πόρνες, σκυλιά, χρηματιστές, φυλακές, ὑγρασία, μεθυσμένοι·
τυφλοί, ζητιάνοι, μιά κιθάρα, τό δέντρο, οἱ κρεμασμένοι, ὁ
   φανοστάτης

Ἀνάμεσα σέ δυό φουγάρα ἕνα ἄστρο. Εὐχαριστῶ.
Τό κλειδί τὄχω ἀφήσει στήν ἴδια θέση πού ἤξερες.

Newspapers, revolts, denials, discoveries, marriages, deaths;
sweat, dust, darkness, all-night drugstore;
a ladder rises blindly; robberies, crimes, injustice;
whores, dogs, brokers, prisons, humidity, drunks;
blind men, beggars, a guitar, the tree, the hanged men, the
    lamppost.

Between two tall chimneys a star. Thank you.
I've left the key in the same place you knew about.

Κάθησαν χάμου, ἀντικρυστά, μές στό χωράφι,
ἔβγαλαν τά παπούτσια τους, κι ἔτσι γυμνά τά πέλματά τους
ἀγγίχτηκαν μές στό ψηλό χορτάρι. Κι ἀπομεῖναν.

They sat down in the field facing each other,
took off their shoes, and bare like that, their soles
touched in the tall grass. And they stayed.

Τό πρόσωπό σου εἶταν κρυμμένο μές στά φύλλα.
Ἔκοβα ἕνα-ἕνα τά φύλλα γιά νά σέ πλησιάσω.
Ὅταν ἔκοψα τό τελευταῖο φύλλο εἶχες φύγει. Τότε
μέ τά κομμένα φύλλα ἔπλεξα ἕνα στεφάνι. Δέν εἶχα
σέ ποιόν νά τό χαρίσω. Τό κρέμασα στό μέτωπό μου.

Your face was hidden in the leaves.
I cut the leaves one by one to get near you.
When I cut the last leaf, you were gone. Then
out of the cut leaves I wove a wreath. I didn't have
anyone to give it to. I hung it on my forehead.

Τά χέρια της ἀκόμη νέα, βασανισμένα
ἀπ' τήν ἀναμονή κι ἀπ' τό διπλάσιο χρόνο,
χλωμά πάνω στό μαῦρο φόρεμά της. Καθόταν
μονάχη στήν αὐλή, μοναχικά κοιτάζοντας
τά καράβια πού χάνονταν. Ἄξαφνα
ἄστραψε ὅλο τό λιόγερμα πάνω στό δαχτυλίδι της
ὅπως τά τζάμια ἑνός χωριοῦ πάνω στό λόφο.
Σκέπασε τότε τρυφερά τό δαχτυλίδι της μέ τήν ἄλλη παλάμη,
ἔκλεισε πρῶτα τά μάτια της, καί μετά χαμογέλασε.

Her hands still young, tormented
by expectation and by twofold time,
pale against her black dress. She was sitting
alone in the courtyard, gazing in isolation
at the ships that were vanishing. Suddenly
all the sunset sparkled on her ring
as on the windows of a village high on the hill.
She then covered the ring tenderly with her other palm,
closed her eyes first, then smiled.

Ἄρχισαν οἱ μεγάλες ὑγρασίες. Οἱ παραθεριστές, ἔφυγαν.
Ἡ πινακίδα τοῦ ξενοδοχείου ξεθωριασμένη, κίτρινη
μέ τόν τίτλο γαλάζιο, κρεμασμένο κάτω ἀπό δυό σύννεφα.
Ἀπό κεῖ περνοῦσε τά πρωϊνά ἀργοπορημένη ἡ καθαρίστρια
πρός τά δωμάτια τῶν νεόνυμφων μέ τίς μακριές κουρτίνες
καί τίς παντοῦφλες τους ζεστές ἀκόμη κάτω ἀπ᾽ τά κρεββάτια.

The great dampness has set in. The vacationers have left.
The hotel sign faded now, yellow
with the name in blue, hung under two clouds.
The cleaning woman would go by there slowly in the mornings
on her way to the rooms of the newly married, with their long
    curtains
and their slippers still warm under the beds.

Ὁ ὑδραυλικός μέ τή γαλάζια φόρμα του πάνω στή σκάλα.
Τά πέλματά του φαρδιά. Οἱ σωλῆνες τῆς θερμάστρας
λάμπουν στό πάτωμα σάν κορμοί δέντρων
ἀπό 'να δάσος ἀσημένιο. Πάνω, στόν τοῖχο,
ἄναψε τό τσιγάρο του. Τό σφυρί του χτυπάει
ἀνάμεσα σέ μικρές κόκκινες λάμψεις. Τί τή θέλαμε
τέτοια ἐποχή τήν ἐγκατάσταση τῆς σόμπας; Ὅπου νᾶναι
καλοκαιριάζει πιά. Κι ἄρχισαν κιόλας νά γεννᾶνε οἱ κόττες
κάτι γαλάζια ρωμαλέα αὐγά, πλάι στό βαρέλι καί τ'ἀλέτρι.

The plumber in his blue overalls on the ladder.
The soles of his feet broad. The pipes of the heating stove
shine on the floor like the trunks of trees
from a silver forest. Up there, against the wall,
he lit his cigarette. His hammer strikes
among small red sparks. What business did we have
putting in a heating stove at this point? Any day now
summer will be here. And the chickens have already begun to lay
some sturdy blue eggs beside the wine barrel and the plough.

Καθώς γράφει, χωρίς νά κοιτάζει τή θάλασσα,
νιώθει νά τρέμει τό μολύβι του ἄκρη-ἄκρη —
εἶναι ἡ στιγμή πού ἀνάβουν οἱ φάροι.

As he writes, without looking at the sea,
he feels his pencil trembling at the very tip—
it's the moment when the lighthouses light up.

Οἱ *νύχτες φεύγουν μέ πλατιούς διασκελισμούς. Γι' αὐτό τά ὡραιότερα ἀγάλματα στέκονται μέ τά πόδια ἐνωμένα.*

The nights leave with broad strides. That's why
the lovelier statues stand with feet together.

The Distant, 1975

Μετρήσαμε τὸν τόπο· ρίξαμε τοὺς νεκροὺς στὸν ἀσβέστη·
ὕστερα μπήκαμε στὴ βάρκα κάτω ἀπ' τὸ λιγοστὸ φεγγάρι·
ὁ τέταρτος κρατοῦσε τὸ σιδερένιο κουτὶ στὰ γόνατά του
συμμαζεμένος ὅλος μέσα του σὰ νὰ ζεσταίνονταν
σὲ μιὰ δική του μυστικὴ φωτιά. Ὁ καπνὸς
στεκόταν χαμηλὰ στὸ νερό, δὲν ἀνέβαινε πάνω.

We measured the place; we threw the dead into the lime;
afterwards we boarded the boat under the slimmest of moons;
the fourth carried the iron box on his knees
huddled in on himself as though taking warmth
from a secret fire of his own. The smoke
stayed low over the water, it didn't rise.

«Εὐρυδίκη», φώναξε. Κατέβηκε γρήγορα τὴ σκάλα.
Τὸ θυρωρεῖο δὲν εἶχε φῶς. Ἔψαξε μὲ τὰ χέρια τὸν καθρέφτη.
Στὸ βάθος ἔφευγε ἡ γυναίκα μὲ τὴν κίτρινη ὀμπρέλα.
Ἡ δεύτερη γυναίκα στὸ ὑπόγειο τοῦ φώναξε: «εἶναι πεθαμένη».
Οἱ τρεῖς ἀεροπόροι βγῆκαν ἀπ' τὸ ἀσανσὲρ μὲ μιὰ μεγάλη
    βαλίτσα—
κεῖ μέσα εἶταν τὰ δυὸ κομμένα χέρια της καὶ τὰ χειρόγραφά
    μου.

"Eurydice," he called. He ran down the stairs.

There was no light in the entrance hall. He searched the mirror
with his hands.

At the far end the woman with the yellow umbrella was leaving.

The second woman in the basement called out to him: "She's
dead."

The three airmen emerged from the elevator with a huge
suitcase—

inside it were her two severed hands and my manuscripts.

Ὁ οὐρανὸς καιγόταν ἔρημος πίσω ἀπ' τὰ σπίτια.
Γιατί κλαῖς ;— ρώτησε δένοντας τὴ ζώνη του.
Εἶναι ὄμορφος ὁ κόσμος — ἀποκρίθηκε ἐκείνη —
τόσο ὄμορφος, μὲ τόσο πονοκέφαλο· καὶ τὸ κρεββάτι
εἶναι ἕνα ἀμίλητο, ἄγριο ζῶο ποὺ ἑτοιμάζεται νὰ φύγει.

The sky burned desolate behind the houses.
Why are you crying? he asked, buckling his belt.
The world is beautiful, she answered,
so beautiful, with such an awful headache; and the bed
is a silent, fierce animal getting ready to leave.

Ἐπειδὴ τὰ λεωφορεῖα εἶταν σταματημένα μπροστὰ στὸ
κιγκλίδωμα
ἐπειδὴ χειρονομοῦσαν οἱ κοῦκλες στὶς φωτισμένες βιτρίνες
ἐπειδὴ τὸ κορίτσι μὲ τὸ ποδήλατο καθυστεροῦσε ἔξω ἀπ᾽ τὸ
φαρμακεῖο
ἐπειδὴ ὁ ξυλουργὸς ἔσπασε τὴν τζαμόπορτα τῆς μπυραρίας
ἐπειδὴ τὸ παιδὶ εἶταν μόνο στὸ ἀσανσὲρ μ᾽ ἕνα κλεμμένο
μολύβι
ἐπειδὴ τὰ σκυλιὰ εἶχαν ἐγκαταλειφθεῖ στὶς παραθαλάσσιες
ἐπαύλεις
ἐπειδὴ ὁ σκουριασμένος τρίφτης εἶχε ἀποσκεπαστεῖ ἀπ᾽ τὶς
τσουκνίδες
ἐπειδὴ ὁ οὐρανὸς εἶταν σταχτὴς μ᾽ ἕνα κόκκινο ψάρι
ἐπειδὴ τὸ ἄλογο στὸ βουνὸ εἶταν πιὸ μόνο ἀπ᾽ τὸ ἄστρο
ἐπειδὴ κι αὐτοὶ κ᾽ ἐκεῖνοι εἶταν κυνηγημένοι
γι᾽ αὐτό, μόνο γι᾽ αὐτό, σᾶς εἶπα ψέματα.

Because the buses were stopped in front of the railing
because the dolls in the lighted shop windows gesticulated
because the girl with the bicycle lingered outside the drugstore
because the carpenter broke the glass door of the beer hall
because the child was alone in the elevator with a stolen pencil
because the dogs had abandoned the seaside villas
because the rusty grater had been covered over by nettles
because the sky was ashen with a red fish
because the horse on the mountain was more alone than the star
because these and those both were hunted
because of this, only because of this, I told you lies.

Τὸ ξέρεις, δὲν ὑπάρχει θάνατος, — τῆς εἶπε.
Τὸ ξέρω, ναί, μιὰ κ' εἶμαι πεθαμένη — ἀπάντησε.
Τὰ δυὸ πουκάμισά σου εἶναι σιδερωμένα στὸ συρτάρι,
μονάχα ἕνα μικρὸ τριαντάφυλλο μοῦ λείπει.

You know, death doesn't exist, he said to her.
I know, yes, now that I'm dead, she answered.
Your two shirts are ironed, in the drawer,
the only thing I'm missing is a small rose.

Ἡ γυναίκα εἶταν ἀκόμα πλαγιασμένη στὸ κρεββάτι. Αὐτὸς ἔβγαλε τὸ γυάλινο μάτι του, τὸ ἀκούμπησε στὸ τραπέζι, ἔκανε ἕνα βῆμα, σταμάτησε. Τώρα μὲ πιστεύεις; — τῆς εἶπε. Ἐκείνη πῆρε τὸ γυάλινο μάτι, τόφερε στὸ μάτι της· τὸν κοίταξε.

The woman was still lying on the bed. He
took out his glass eye, set it down on the table,
took a step, stopped. Now do you believe me? he said to her.
She picked up the glass eye, brought it close to her eye; she looked
    at him.

Μικρά, ἀεικίνητα τετράγωνα εἰσδύοντας τόνα μέσα στ' ἄλλο,
βγαίνοντας τόνα μὲς ἀπ' τ' ἄλλο, χτίζοντας, ξεχτίζοντας
μιὰ πολιτεία παράθυρα - παράθυρα· δεξιὰ κι ἀριστερὰ οἱ δύο
    γωνίες
ὀρθωμένες ἀσύμμετρα κι ἀμέσως ὕστερα
ἀθόρυβη ἡ μεγάλη κατάρρευση μὲς στὴν ἀθόρυβη κίνηση, ἐνῶ
τὰ τρία λιγνὰ σκυλιὰ ξεμάκραιναν μὲς ἀπ' τὰ διαδοχικὰ
    τετράγωνα
ὀσμίζοντας ξένους νεκροὺς καὶ τὰ μεγάλα ραβδιά τους ὡς
    τὸ βάθος
ἐκεῖ ποὺ ἡ γυναίκα γυμνὴ σηκώνει τὸ γδαρμένο λαγὸ μπροστὰ
    στὸν καθρέφτη.

Small squares in perpetual motion, one penetrating the other,
one emerging from the other: building, unbuilding,
a city of windows on windows; right and left the two corners
rising asymmetrically and just beyond,
noiseless, the great collapse in the midst of noiseless motion, while
the three lean dogs grew more distant in the successive squares
smelling foreign dead and their great staves to the far end,
there where the woman, naked, raises the skinned hare in front of
    a mirror.

Τέσσερα στρογγυλά, γυμνὰ τραπέζια κατὰ μῆκος τῆς
   στενόμακρης αἴθουσας·
τὸ φῶς ἔπεφτε πάνω τους σταχτί, βροχερὸ ἀπ᾽ τὴ μεγάλη
   τζαμαρία·
δίπλα στὸ δεύτερο τραπέζι, ἀμέτοχος, σχεδὸν ἐχθρικός,
   στεκόταν ὁ μονόχειρας·
τὸ χέρι του εἶταν κατακόκκινο· κρατοῦσε ἕνα μικρό, πορτοκαλὶ
   βιβλίο· —
ὅλο τὸ βάρος ἔπεφτε στὸ ποὺ δὲν ξέραμε διόλου τὴ συνέχεια.

Four round, bare tables the length of the long and narrow hall;
the light hit them like ash, rainy through the large plate-glass
    window;
beside the second table, not taking part, almost hostile, stood the
    one-armed man;
his arm was all red; he was holding a small orange book—
the whole point was that we didn't know at all what would
    follow.

Ἄκουσες τὴ φωνή σου νὰ λέει: ε ὐ χ α ρ ι σ τ ῶ —
(τόσο ἀπροσδόκητη, βουβὴ φυσικότητα) — εἴσουν βέβαιος
   πιά:
ἕνα μεγάλο κομμάτι αἰωνιότητα σοῦ ἀνῆκε.

You heard your voice saying: *thanks*
(so unexpected, dumb naturalness)—you were certain now:
a large piece of eternity belonged to you.

Οἱ μεθυσμένοι πλαγιάσαν· κοιμηθῆκαν ἀμέσως. Ἐκεῖνος
κοίταξε τοὺς λογαριασμούς, ἔσβησε τὸ φῶς, βγῆκε στὸν κῆπο.
Ἔνιωσε κάτω ἀπ' τὸ παπούτσι του τὴ στρογγυλὴ ἀπαλότητα
    ἑνὸς μπουμπουκιοῦ.
Ἄ, μακρινὸ λησμονημένο ἀπερίφραχτο· ὦ μάντεμα,
σταγόνα κρυφῆς φεγγαρόβρυσης σ' ἕνα μονάχα φύλλο. Κι
    ἄξαφνα
ἀνάψαν καὶ τὰ ἑφτὰ παράθυρα πίσω ἀπ' τὰ δέντρα. Οἱ
    μεθυσμένοι
ὀρθοὶ στὰ κρεββάτια τους δεῖχναν ὁ ἕνας στὸν ἄλλον τὰ
    ὄργανά τους σὲ στύση.

The drunk ones lay down; they fell asleep immediately. He
looked over the accounts, turned out the light, went out into the
   garden.
He felt under his shoe the round softness of a bud.
O distant, you who are forgotten, unfenced; O divination,
a drop from a secret moon-fountain on a single leaf. And suddenly
all seven windows lit up behind the trees. The drunk ones,
standing on their beds, were showing each other their erections.

Ἄκουσε ποὺ φωνάζαν τ' ὄνομά του πάνω ἀπ' τὰ νερά.
Βεβαιώθηκε πὼς εἶταν γι' αὐτόν. Κρύφτηκε.
Ἕνα ὀγκῶδες κατάφωτο καράβι ἔβγαινε ἀπ' τὸ λιμάνι.
Στὴ γέφυρα ἡ γυναίκα μ' ἕνα τεράστιο δαντελένιο καπέλο.
Σκεπάστηκαν ὁ σκοτεινὸς πύργος, τὸ φεγγάρι, τὸ ἰκρίωμα.

He heard them calling his name over the water.
He verified that it was for him. He hid.
A huge brightly lit ship emerged from the harbor.
On the bridge the woman with an enormous lace hat.
It blocked the dark tower from view, the moon, the scaffold.

Χλωμός, πολὺ χλωμός· ἀγκάθια στὰ μαλλιά του—ἀγκάθια
πολὺ μακριὰ ὣς τοὺς ὤμους, ὣς τὴ μέση, ὣς τὰ πέλματα—
ἴσως καὶ νᾶταν τὰ ἴδια τὰ φτερά του· γιατὶ μόλις
ἔκανα δεύτερη φορὰ νὰ δῶ κατὰ τὴν πόρτα, δὲν ὑπῆρχε
πάρεξ ὁ ἐλάχιστος καπνὸς στὴ θέση τοῦ σφυριοῦ.

Pale, very pale; thorns in his hair—thorns
down to his shoulders, to his waist, to the soles of his feet—
maybe they were actually his wings; because just
as I glanced a second time toward the door, there was nothing
but the slightest smoke in place of the hammer.

Ρίχτε τὸν προβολέα κατευθείαν στὸ πρόσωπό του·
ἔτσι κρυμμένος μὲς στὴ νύχτα νὰ φαίνεται, νὰ λάμπει·
ἔχει ὄμορφα δόντια—τὸ ξέρει· χαμογελάει
μὲ τὸ μικρὸ φεγγάρι πάνω στὸν βομβαρδισμένο λόφο,
μὲ τὰ παιδιὰ τῶν ξυλοκόπων κάτω στὸ ποτάμι.

Throw the spotlight right on his face;
hidden like this in the night, let's see him, make him glow;
he has beautiful teeth—and he knows it; he smiles
with the small moon up on the bombed-out hill,
with the children of the woodcutters down by the river.

Τόσο καὶ τόσο μακρινό, — γι᾽ αὐτὸ καὶ ἄτρωτο — εἶπε·
ὡστόσο κανένας ἀρκετὰ μακρινός· κανένας ὅσο τὸ θέλει,
ὅσο ἴσως καὶ θὰ τὸ μπορούσε ἢ ὅσο πρέπει.
Μὲ τὸ μαντίλι του τυλίγει τὸν καρπὸ τοῦ χεριοῦ του
βουβά, καμμιὰ χειρονομία, οὔτε κόκκινο οὔτε μαῦρο·
ἄσπρο μαντίλι, τὸ πυκνότερο, τὸ μακρινότερο ἄσπρο.

So very very distant—and therefore invulnerable too—he said;
yet no one distant enough; no one as much as he would like,
as much maybe as he could be or should be.
With his handkerchief he wraps his wrist
dumb, no gesture at all, neither red nor black;
white handkerchief: the densest, most distant white.

Γήϊνο βάθος σκοτεινὸ ὡς τὸ τέλος. Ἕνα μόνο
παράθυρο ἀναμμένο—ἕνα μεγάλο
κλεμμένο πράσινο διαμάντι. Ὁ οὐρανὸς
ὁλόλευκος, ὁλόγυμνος. Ὢ μυστικὸ ξημέρωμα—εἶπε—
δέρμα λευκὸ κατάστικτο μὲ κόκκινους πόρους· ὄνειρο,
ὄνειρο ἐπουλωμένα, ἡ οὐλή σου πιὸ λευκὴ στὸν κρόταφό μας.

Earthly depth dark to the end. Only one
window lit—a large
stolen green diamond. The sky
all white, all naked. O secret daybreak, he said—
white skin stippled with red pores; dream,
healed dream, your scar whiter at our temples.

Μπαοῦλα καὶ μπαοῦλα, καὶ τὸ βιολὶ ἀφημένο στὸ κρεββάτι
καὶ τὸ μαῦρο καὶ τ' ἄσπρο σὲ πυκνοὺς διασταυρούμενους
    ρόμβους
κ' ἡ πρώτη γριὰ μὲ τὰ χοντρὰ διάτρητα ὀπίσθια
καὶ τριαντάφυλλα καὶ τσιγάρα κ' ἕνα τυφλὸ μαργαριτάρι
κ' ἕνα μικρὸ χρυσοκέντητο φαντὸ πάνω στὸ πιάνο —
μὲς στοὺς καπνοὺς ἐπιπλέαν τὰ εὐγενέστερα χέρια,
καμιόνια κατάφορτα πολεμοφόδια τρέχαν στὶς ὑπόγειες
    γαλαρίες,
ἐσὺ καθισμένος στὸ πάτωμα ξεφλούδιζες φυστίκια
καὶ μπὰμ καὶ μπούμ, κ' οἱ νεκροὶ εἶταν πιὸ μέσα καὶ πιὸ πάνω.

More footlockers, more trunks, and the violin abandoned on the
    bed,
black and white both in dense crossed rhombuses
and the first crone with the fat, riddled rear end
and roses and cigarettes and a blind pearl
and a small gold-laced embroidery on the piano—
in the smoke the noblest hands floated,
trucks heavy with military supplies rumbled along underground
    passages,
you sitting on the floor shelling peanuts
and BAM and BOOM, and the dead were farther in and farther
    up.

Κάτι δὲν πάει καλὰ μὲ τὴ γιορτὴ ποὺ μοῦ ἑτοιμάζουν.
Ἀνεβοκατεβαίνουν σκάλες, συνωθοῦνται στοὺς διαδρόμους.
Οἱ τρεῖς πολυέλαιοι τῆς μεγάλης αἴθουσας ἄναψαν.
Πάνω στὴν ἕδρα λάμπει τὸ ποτήρι τὸ νερό. Μὲ ἀναγγέλλουν.
Σπρώχνω τὰ πόδια μου· ψάχνομαι μὲ τὰ χέρια· λείπω.
Κι ἂν κάνω νὰ κατέβω τὴ σκάλα θὰ μὲ συλλάβει ὁ κλητήρας.

Something has gone wrong with the celebration they're preparing
   for me.
They go up and down stairs, jostle each other in the corridors.
The three chandeliers in the large hall have come on.
Up on the podium the glass of water glows. They announce me.
I urge my feet; search myself with my hands; I'm missing.
And if I try to go down the stairs, the usher will arrest me.

Αὐτὴ ἡ ἀπεριόριστη ἐπανάληψη τοῦ ἴδιου δυσανάγνωστου
κειμένου —
στὸ πάνω μέρος τῆς σελίδας ἡ σκουριασμένη τρύπα ἀπ' τὸ
καρφί,
στὸ κάτω μέρος δυὸ σταγόνες μαῦρο αἷμα. Τὸ δύο — εἶπε —
τὸ δύο,
τὸ διπλό, τὸ διπλόηχο, τὸ διπλονόητο. Κουράστηκα μὲ τὶς
πόρτες
κλειστὲς ἢ ἀνοιχτὲς μὲ νεκροὺς ἢ γυναῖκες. Ὁ Λευτέρης
ἔφυγε βιαστικὰ γιὰ νὰ προλάβει πρὶν πιάσει ἡ βροχή.
Ὕστερα γύρισε μὲ τὴ βρεγμένη κουβέρτα καὶ τὴν τραγιάσκα
τοῦ σκοτωμένου.

This relentless repetition of the same illegible text—
at the top of the sheet the rusted hole from the thumbtack,
at the bottom two drops of black blood. The two—he said—the two,
the double, the double sound, the double meaning. I'm tired of
     doors
closed and open with the dead or women. Lefteris
got going in a hurry before it started raining.
Afterwards he came back with the damp blanket and the cap
     belonging to the one who was executed.

Άνετη ἐφαρμογὴ τοῦ σώματος σὲ κάθε του στάση, κάθε ὥρα,
σὲ κάθε φωτισμό, τὸ ἴδιο καὶ στὰ ἔπιπλα. Ἡ πράσινη πόρτα
στὴ σωστὴ θέση της. Τὰ μαλλιά σου βαραῖναν πιότερο ἀπ᾽ τὰ
    βλέφαρά σου.
Δὲν εἶχε σημασία ἂν θ᾽ ἀργοῦσες. Τὸ δεύτερο πουλὶ
εἶπε ὅ,τι καὶ τὸ πρῶτο. Κανένας δὲν κρατάει τὰ κλειδιά του.
    Ἡ Μαρία,
σὰ νάτανε γυμνὴ κι ἀόρατη πάνω ἀπ᾽ τὸ θάνατό της, ἄναψε
    τὸ σπίρτο.
Σὲ λίγο ἀκούστηκαν στὸ κάτω προάστιο οἱ ἐκρήξεις.

Easy accommodation of the body in all its postures, every hour,
in all lighting, the same with the furniture. The green door
in its right place. Your hair fell heavier than your eyelids.
It didn't matter if you'd be late. The second bird
said what the first said. No one holds his own keys. Maria,
as though naked and invisible over her death, lit the match.
In a little while the sound of explosions in the lower suburb.

Ἀκούστηκε ἡ βαθειὰ φωνὴ στὴ βαθύτερη νύχτα.
Ὕστερα πέρασαν τὰ τάνκς. Ὕστερα ξημέρωσε.
Ὕστερα ἀκούστηκε ξανὰ ἡ φωνὴ πιὸ κοντινή, πιὸ μέσα.
Ὁ τοῖχος εἶταν ἄσπρος. Τὸ ψωμὶ κόκκινο. Ἡ σκάλα
στεκόταν κάθετη σχεδὸν στὸν παλιὸ φανοστάτη. Ἡ γριὰ
μάζευε στὴ χαρτοσακκούλα μία - μία τὶς μαῦρες πέτρες.

The deep voice was heard in the deeper night.
Then the tanks went by. Then day broke.
Then the voice was heard again, shorter, farther in.
The wall was white. The bread red. The ladder
rested almost vertical against the antique lamppost. The old
    woman
collected the black stones one by one in a paper bag.

Καθένας μ' ἔναν ἢ καὶ πιότερους νεκροὺς στὴ ράχη του.
Δρόμος καὶ δρόμος, πέτρες, τὰ καδρόνια, ἔνα καμένο δέντρο.
Ἄφησε χάμου τὸ φανάρι· τὸ ψωμὶ στὸ κούτσουρο. Ποῦ τοὺς
    κουβαλᾶτε;
Δὲν ἔχει χῶμα πιὸ πάνω. Δὲ βγαίνει χορτάρι. Τρεῖς μῆνες
τὴ βγάλαμε μόνο μὲ χαρούπια· κ' ἡ θύμηση ἀδειάζει.
Ἄν τόπο δὲν ἔχουν οἱ νεκροί, δὲν ἔχουμε τόπο καὶ μεῖς νὰ
    σταθοῦμε.
Τότες ἀνάψαμε τὶς μεγάλες φωτιές· βάλαμε τὸ γέροντα στὸ
    βράχο·
βγάλαμε τὶς ἀρβύλες μας· κ' ἔτσι κατάχαμα στὸ χῶμα,
δυὸ-δυὸ μετρήσαμε τὰ πόδια μας ἀντικρυστὰ πέλμα μὲ
    πέλμα.
Ὁ μικρὸς Κωνσταντής, ὁ πιὸ μεγαλοπόδαρος, χόρεψε πρῶτος.

Each of them with one or even more deaths on his back.
Road on road, stones, rafters, a burnt tree.
Someone set the lamp down, the bread on a log. Where are you
  carrying the dead?
There's no earth up that way. No grass grows. For three months
we got along on carob beans alone; and memory runs out.
If the dead don't have any territory, we too don't have territory to
  stand on.
Then we lit the great fires; we set the old man on the rock;
we took off our boots; and sitting like this on the ground
two by two we measured our feet, soles against soles.
Young Konstandis, who had the largest feet, danced first.

Ψήσαμε τὶς πατάτες στὴ χόβολη. Μὲ τὸ ἁλάτι, στὰ δυὸ
δάχτυλα ἀκόμη,
ἀκούσαμε τὸ σκούξιμο στὴν αὐλή, πλάϊ στὸ μαγγανοπήγαδο.
Σώπα—εἶπε·—
νὰ φύγεις ἀπ᾽ τὸν πίσω φράχτη. Πάρε τὴν κουβέρτα. Ἕνα
κίβδηλο φεγγάρι
ἀπὸ τζάμι σὲ τζάμι, ἀπὸ στέγη σὲ στέγη, κι ὁ καθρέφτης
μέσα στὴ ντουλάπα
προδοτικός, μὲ μάτια δεμένα· πιὸ μέσα εἶταν τὰ ροῦχα τῶν
νεκρῶν
μὲ τ᾽ ἀχρησιμοποίητα εἰσιτήρια στὶς τσέπες. Σιωπηλὴ
ἀνεξαρτησία
ἀπ᾽ τοὺς δικούς μας φόβους κι ἀπ᾽ τὰ καλύτερα ὄνειρα. Τὸ
ἄγαλμα
ἐκεῖ στὴν εἴσοδο παραληροῦσε μὲ τὸ πρόσωπο κόκκινο ἀπ᾽
τὴ δική του ἡδονή. Τότε
ἀκούστηκε τὸ ἀλύχτημα τῶν σκύλων. Γλύτωσαν λοιπόν. Εἶχαν
περάσει τὸ ποτάμι.

We roasted the potatoes in the embers. With the salt still between
    our fingers
we heard the howling in the yard, near the wheel-well. Quiet, he
    said,
leave through the rear fence. Take the blanket. A counterfeit
    moon
from window to window, from roof to roof, and the mirror in the
    wardrobe
traitorous, with eyes blindfolded; farther inside hung the clothes of
    the dead
with the unused tickets in the pockets. Silent independence
from our own fears and from the better dreams. The statue
there in the entrance hall raved, its face red from its own
    sensuality. Then
the sound of the dogs barking. So they got away. They'd crossed
    the river.

Ἔδεσε τὸ σκοινὶ στὸ δέντρο. Στὸ σκοινὶ
δὲν ἔδεσε τίποτα· τ᾽ ἄφησε κάτω στὸ χῶμα
γιὰ κείνους ποὺ πηδοῦν τὸ πρωὶ τὰ ποτάμια
γιὰ κείνους ποὺ πηδοῦν τὴ νύχτα ἀπὸ στέγη σὲ στέγη· —
κάτι ἀπ τὴν τσέπη τους θὰ πέσει, ὅσο καλὰ φυλαγμένο·
οἱ ὁδοκαθαριστὲς τὴν ἄλλη μέρα θὰ τὸ βροῦνε
καὶ ἡ ἐντολὴ ἀμετάκλητη: νὰ τὸ προσκομίσουν —

(κάτι τὸ γενικὸ χρειαζόταν πάντοτε στὸ τέλος).

He tied the rope to the tree. He didn't tie anything
to the rope; he let it lie on the ground
for those who vault the river in the morning
for those who vault from roof to roof at night—
something will fall out of their pockets, however well protected;
the street cleaners will find it the following day
and their orders will be irrevocable: they must hand it over—

(something general was always needed in the end)

Μιὰ φούχτα κόκκαλα κ' ἕνα κομμάτι σκουριασμένο σίδερο.
  Ἡ γυναίκα
μάζευε χόρτα στὸν ἀγρὸ — φαινόνταν ὡς πάνω τὰ πόδια της.
  Πιὸ κεῖ
τὸ σκυλὶ φρουροῦσε τὸ βρέφος   κάτω ἀπ' τὸ δέντρο. Μόλις
  βράδιασε
γυρίσαμε στὴν πολιτεία, σταθήκαμε μπροστὰ στὸ κόκκινο
  σπίτι,
κοιτάξαμε ἀπ' τὸ χαμηλὸ παράθυρο. Οἱ δύο στὸ τραπέζι, πλάϊ
  στὴ λάμπα·
τὰ πιάτα τοῦ δείπνου· ἀργὲς κινήσεις — μιὰ σιωπηλὴ μνησι-
  κακία. Ὁ τρίτος ὄρθιος
στεκόταν πάνω τους μ' ἕνα μαχαίρι καθαρίζοντας τὸ μῆλο.
  Κείνη τὴ στιγμὴ
γύρισε κ' εἶπε: στὸ ἴδιο καταλήγουμε πάντα· κ' ἴσως μ' αὐτὸ
  νὰ ἐννοοῦσε
τὴν πρώτη ἁμαρτία ἢ τὸ ποὺ εἶχε ξεχάσει τὴ χτένα του στὸν
  ξένο λουτήρα.

A handful of bones and a piece of rusted iron. The woman
was gathering greens in the field—her legs exposed all the way up.
   Beyond,
the dog guarded the infant under the tree. As soon as it became
   dark
we returned to the town, stopped in front of the red house,
looked through the low window. The two of them at the table,
   beside the lamp;
the supper plates; slow movements—a silent rancor. The third
standing over them with a knife, peeling an apple. That second
he turned and said: we always end up with the same thing; and by
   that he may have meant
the first sin or his having forgotten his comb in somebody else's
   bathroom.

Φανοστάτες πεσμένοι· κ' ἔνα δέντρο· — τὸ φῶς κυκλοφοροῦσε
     ἀπὸ κάτω·
τὸ δεύτερο πέρασμα δίπλα στοὺς ὑπονόμους. Φέραν τὰ
     βίντζια,
σηκῶσαν τὰ βαγόνια, πῆραν τοὺς νεκρούς. Δὲ φταίξαμε —
     εἶπε.
'Ανάμεσα στὶς σιδηροτροχιὲς ἡ γριὰ μάζευε χαμομήλια.
Βρῆκε τὸ ρολόϊ τοῦ εἰσαγγελέα· τὸ πέρασε στὸ χέρι της. Τί
     θαρρεῖς, γιέ μου,
ποὺ οἱ νεκροὶ δὲν πεινᾶνε ; — τρῶνε τὰ σίδερα, τὶς πόρτες,
     τὴν πέτρα. Τότε
πάνω ἀπ' τὸ πρόχωμα φώναξε ὁ Βαγγέλης. Δὲν ξεχώρισαν·
     λόγια. Οἱ ἄλλοι
βγάλαν ἀπ' τὰ πουκάμισά τους τὶς σημαῖες καὶ προχωρῆσαν
     πρὸς τὸν χάλκινο ἱππέα.

Fallen lampposts; and a tree—the light circulated from below;
the second passage along the sewer. They brought the cranes,
raised the coaches, took the dead. It wasn't our fault, he said.
Between the tracks the old woman was gathering camomile flowers.
She found the prosecutor's watch; she slipped it on her wrist. You
    think, my son,
that the dead don't get hungry? They eat iron, doors, stone. Then,
above the retaining wall, Vangelis shouted. They couldn't make out
    words. The others
brought the flags out from under their shirts and moved on toward
    the bronze horseman.

Εἶταν ποὺ κοιτούσαμε κι ἀπ' τὶς δύο μεριές, — ὁ χρόνος
ἰσοζυγιαζόταν κάπως —
ὁ μέσα καθρέφτης καὶ τὸ δέντρο καὶ τὸ περίπτερο τοῦ
ἀνάπηρου. Ὧρες κι ὧρες
πολύχρωμα περιοδικὰ κ' ἐφημερίδες — τὰ γυμνά, ὁ καπνός,
οἱ σκοτωμένοι, χαράδρες·
ἐτούτη ἡ σκοτεινὴ ἀνωνυμία· κ' οἱ τοῖχοι ἀπέναντι, φωτισμένοι.
Ἡδονή, — φώναζε ἡ γυναίκα — κόκκινη ἡδονὴ μὲ κόκκινα
νύχια,
κόκκινο σῶμα σφαγμένο· καὶ τὸ σεντόνι κρεμάμενο ὣς κάτω
στὴν πέτρινη σκάλα
κ' οἱ τρεῖς ὡραῖοι νέοι, πιασμένοι ὦμο - ὦμο (ὁ μεσαῖος εἶταν
ἄγαλμα)
νὰ σεργιανᾶνε ἀπρόθυμα μέσα στὴ λιόλουστη ἀμεριμνησία
τοῦ θανάτου.

It was that we looked at both sides—time fell into a certain
    balance—
the inside mirror and the tree and the disabled veteran's kiosk.
    Hour on hour
multicolored magazines and newspapers—the nudes, smoke, those
    killed, ravines;
this dark anonymity; and the walls opposite: lit up.
Pleasure, yelled the woman, red pleasure with red fingernails,
red body slaughtered; and the sheet hanging down to the stone
    stairway
and the three handsome young men, linked shoulder to shoulder
    (the one in the middle a statue),
strolling reluctantly in the sunlit insouciance of death.

Αὐτὸ ποὺ δὲν ἀπαιτεῖ κι οὔτε ἔχει ἀποδείξεις. Ἕνα πρᾶο,
    ἀσυμπλήρωτο φεγγάρι
τρυπώντας μὲ τόνα του δάχτυλο τὸν τοῖχο. Ἀπὸ μέσα ὁ
    καθρέφτης
ἔψαχνε μιὰ κατάφαση στὸ πρόσωπό μας. Ἐσὺ κοιτοῦσες
    ἀλλοῦ.
Χτυπῆσαν τὴν πόρτα. Τοὺς ἄνοιξες. Δὲ μίλησαν. Μᾶς
    κοίταξαν
σὰ νἄμαστε ἐμεῖς ποὖχαμε κάνει λάθος. Φύγαν. Στὸ κάτω
    σκαλοπάτι,
εἶχαν ἀφήσει τ᾽ ἄλλα τρία καρφιά, τὸ σφυρὶ καὶ τὸ ποίημα,
    Στὸν κῆπο
τὸ λιγοστὸ φεγγάρι εἶχε μεταφερθεῖ πίσω ἀπ᾽ τ᾽αὐτὶ τοῦ
    ἀγάλματος. Εἶχε ἀκούσει.

This that doesn't demand and doesn't even have receipts. A calm,
    incomplete moon
piercing the wall with one finger. From inside, the mirror
searched for a confirmation in our faces. You were looking
    elsewhere.
They knocked on the door. You opened it for them. They didn't
    say anything. They stared at us
as though we were the ones who'd made a mistake. They left. On
    the step below,
they'd left the other three nails, the hammer and the poem. In the
    garden
the sliver of a moon had moved behind the statue's ear. It had
    heard.

Μπορεῖς νὰ τὸ ἐπιτύχεις μᾶλλον εὔκολα—ἀρκεῖ
νὰ μὴ θέλεις νὰ πείσεις ἢ ν' ἀπατήσεις. Μόνα καὶ μόνα
τὰ πουλιά, τὰ παιδιά, ἡ μουσική, ὁ καναπές, οἱ κουρτίνες.
Ἡ ἄρρωστη γυναίκα σιδερώνει. Μιὰ τελευταία μύγα
σχεδὸν ἑτοιμοθάνατη σεργιανάει στὸ ζεσταμένο σεντόνι.
Κ' ὑπάρχουν μυστικὲς ἀλληλουχίες μὲ μειλίχιους νεκροὺς
πιὸ πέρα ἀπ' τὸν κοινό μας θάνατο, πέρ' ἀπ' τ' ἀγάλματά του
εὐγενικὰ καὶ ὑμνητικὰ μέσα στὸ φευγαλέο ἐκεῖνο θαῦμα,
μέσα στὸ φέγγος αὐτοῦ τοῦ καθρέφτη ποὺ ξέρει ν' ἀντιγράφει
(ὅσο πλαστὰ κι ἀποσπασματικὰ) τὴ δόξα δυὸ γυμνῶν
    σωμάτων.

You can accomplish it rather easily—it's enough
not to want to persuade or deceive. Alone and alone
the birds, the children, the music, the couch, the curtains.
The sick woman is ironing. A last fly
almost ready to die wanders along the warm sheet.
And there are secret sequences with mild deaths
beyond our common death, beyond its statues
polite and laudatory within that fleeting miracle,
within the light of this mirror that knows how to copy
(however false and fragmentary) the glory of two naked bodies.

Ψάχνοντας πάλι καὶ πάλι ἀπ' τὴν ἀρχὴ γιὰ κεῖνο τὸ ἀπέραντα
    λεῖο,
γιὰ κεῖνο τὸ βαθιὰ στρογγυλό, — λίθος λευκὸς τῆς λησμονιᾶς
    φυλαγμένος
στὴ μαύρη ναυτικὴ κασέλα. Ἡ γυναίκα εἶχε σκύψει στὸ
    παράθυρο
πιέζοντας στὸ ξύλο τὸν ἀριστερὸ μαστό της. Στὸ λούκι
τῆς ἀπέναντι στέγης εἶταν σταματημένη ἡ κόκκινη σφαίρα.
Αὐτὸ σκεφτόμουν — εἶπε, ἀκούγοντας μὲ θλίψη τὴν φωνή της
    τὴν ἴδια,
κοιτάζοντας τὸ ἄγαλμα κάτω στὸν κῆπο — αὐτὸ ποὺ ἀνασύραν
προχτὲς τὸ βράδι ἀπ' τὴ θάλασσα μὲ τὶς πολλὲς ἀσετυλίνες.
    Πῶς ἀνεβαίνει
φαρδύς, νωπὸς ὁ ἀντίχειράς του στὰ νωπά του χείλη
φράζοντας τὸ θαυμάσιο περιληπτικὸ λευκὸ προτοῦ προλάβει
    νὰ ἐκφραστεῖ.

Searching again and again from the beginning for that infinite
    smoothness,
for that deep roundness—white stone of forgetfulness kept
in the black sea chest. The woman had stooped to the window,
pressing her left breast against the wood. The red ball
was stuck in the drainpipe of the roof opposite.
That's what I was thinking about, she said, hearing her own voice
    with sadness,
gazing at the statue in the garden below—that which they brought
    up
night before last out of the sea with all those acetylene torches.
    How it rises
broad, its thumb still damp against its damp lip
blocking the wonderful concise whiteness before it manages to find
    expression.

Ὁ πάγκος τοῦ ἀργυραμοιβοῦ τζαμένιος—τί παράξενα νομι-
σματα, τὶ ὀδοντοστοιχίες
χρυσές, ἀσημένιες, σιδερένιες· καὶ μονὲς κορῶνες νεκρῶν· τὸ
περιδέραιο τῆς Ἑλένης·
μιὰ πελώρια καρφίτσα καπέλου· ἡ Παλαιὰ Διαθήκη
ἀσημόδετη
μὲ κόκκινες καὶ πράσινες πέτρες. Χτυποῦσε δώδεκα τὸ μεγάλο
ρολόϊ τῆς Δημαρχίας.
Βγάζαν ἀπ᾽ τὴν κατάψυξη τὰ πουλερικά. Ὁ στιλβωτὴς
στεκόταν στὴν πόρτα
ἔχοντας περασμένες στὰ χέρια του τὶς μπότες τοῦ Ἀντίνοου.
Τότε
φύσηξε λίγο ἀπ᾽ τὸ νοτιά· σάλεψε τὸ μακρὺ σεντόνι. Κάτω
ἀπ᾽ τὸ κρεββάτι
φάνηκε τὄνα ὁλόλευκο γοβάκι τῆς πεθαμένης νύφης.

The moneychanger's counter made of glass—what strange coins,
   what false teeth
of gold, silver, iron; and single gold teeth of the dead; Eleni's
   necklace;
an enormous hatpin; the Old Testament silver-bound
with red and green stones. The large clock on the town hall struck
   twelve.
They took the poultry out of the freezer. The shoeshine man stood
   at the door
with the boots of Antinoüs slipped over his hands. Then
a little breeze from the south; the long sheet stirred. Under the bed
you could see the dead bride's pure white high-heeled shoe.

Γυμνὰ τ' ἀγάλματα κάτω ἀπ' τὰ δέντρα τῶν νεκροταφείων
πολιορκημένα ἀπ' τὶς παράφορες φωνὲς τῶν βραδινῶν πουλιῶν
ὅταν οἱ τελευταῖοι τῆς πομπῆς ἀποσύρονται. Τ' ἀγάλματα
μιμοῦνται πειστικὰ τὸ θάνατο, τὸν ἔρωτα, τὴν ἠρεμία,
μ' ἕνα μικρὸ σιδερένιο φανάρι στὸ χέρι, μ' ἕνα μαρμάρινο
    κρίνο,
μὲ πέτρινα σπαθιά, μὲ πέτρινες φτεροῦγες, πέτρινες σημαῖες,
ἀπ' τὸ πέρα στὸ ἐδῶ, στὸ ἀλλοῦ· παράθυρα ἀναμμένα·
    κρεββάτια,
νυχτερινὸς χορὸς στὸν κῆπο. Φύγετε, φύγετε, — φώναξε ὁ
    Πέτρος·
ὁ ἐπιστάτης ἔχει τὰ κλειδιά μου στὴ ζώνη του· τὸ σκυλί του
μὲ παίρνει ἀπὸ πίσω· — εἶναι ἡ ἄρνησή μου. Τ' ἀγάλματα
δὲν ἀντιγράφουν ἐμᾶς· εἶναι μόνα κ' ἐκεῖνα· πονοῦν· ἀντι-
    φάσκουν στὴν ἀνυπαρξία,
ἀνάβουν, κοκκινίζουν· ἡ κεντρική τους φλέβα ὀγκώνεται ἀπ'
    τὸ αἷμα.
Γι' αὐτὸ καὶ τὰ πουλιὰ φωνάζουν τόσο — νὰ καλύψουν τὴν
    ἥττα τοῦ καθησυχαστικοῦ θανάτου.

The statues naked under the trees in the cemeteries
besieged by the passionate voices of the night birds
when the last of the procession retires. The statues
faithfully imitate death, sensual love, calm,
with a small iron lamp in hand, with a marble lily,
with stone swords, with stone wings, stone flags,
from far to near to elsewhere; windows lit; beds,
night dance in the garden. Leave, leave, Petros yelled;
the custodian has my keys on his belt; his dog
is following me—it's my rejection of him. The statues
don't copy us; they are alone too; they suffer; they contradict
    nonexistence,
they get excited, blush; their central vein swells with blood.
That's why the birds cry out so: to cover the defeat of serene death.

Ὦ, μακρινό, μακρινό· βαθὺ ἀπλησίαστο· νὰ ὑποδέχεσαι πάντα
τοὺς σιωπηλοὺς μὲς ἀπ᾽ τὴν ἀπουσία τους, μὲς ἀπ᾽ τὴν
ἀπουσία τῶν ἄλλων
ὅταν ὁ κίνδυνος ἀπ᾽ τὸν πλησίον, ἀπ᾽ τὸ πλησίον βαραίνει
σὲ νύχτες ὑποσχετικὲς μὲ πολύχρωμα φῶτα στοὺς κήπους
ὅταν τὰ μάτια τῶν λιονταριῶν καὶ τῶν τίγρεων μισοκλεισμένα
φωσφορίζουν
μὲ πράσινες διακεκομμένες ἀποσιωπήσεις πίσω ἀπ᾽ τὰ κλουβιά
τους
κι ὁ γέρο-γελωτοποιὸς μπροστὰ στὸν σκοτεινὸ καθρέφτη
ξεβάφει τὰ ζωγραφιστά του δάκρυα γιὰ νὰ μπορέσει νὰ
κλάψει—
ὤ, ἥσυχο ἀδώρητο, ἐσὺ μὲ τὸ μακρύ, ὑγραμένο χέρι,
ἥσυχο ἀόρατο χωρὶς δανεισμοὺς καὶ ὑποχρεώσεις
καρφώνοντας καρφιὰ στὸν ἀέρα, στεριώνοντας τὸν κόσμο
μέσα σ᾽ ἐκείνη τὴ βαθειὰ ἀπραξία ποὺ ἡ μουσικὴ βασιλεύει.

O distant, distant; deep unapproachable; receive always
the silent ones in their absence, in the absence of the others
when the danger from the near ones, from the near itself, burdens
during nights of promise with many-colored lights in the gardens,
when the half-closed eyes of lions and tigers scintillate
with flashing green omissions in their cages
and the old jester in front of the dark mirror
washes off his painted tears so that he can weep—
O quiet ungrantable, you with the long, damp hand,
quiet invisible, without borrowing and lending, without obligations,
nailing nails on the air, shoring up the world
in that deep inaction where music reigns.

YANNIS RITSOS: BIOGRAPHICAL DATA

The following is based largely on G. Valetas, "Σχεδίασμα Χρονολογίας Γιάννη Ρίτσου," Αἰολικὰ Γράμματα, Vol. 32-33, May-June 1976, pp. 295-300. Ms. K. Makrynikola of Kedros Publishers also provided helpful suggestions.

1909   Born on May 1 in Monemvasia, Laconia, Greece (his parents were established landowners in the region).
1921   Entered the gymnasium at Gythion, having completed his early schooling in Monemvasia.
1925   Moved to Athens on graduating from secondary school and found work typing and copying legal documents.
1926   Returned to Monemvasia with the first signs of tuberculosis. Began writing poetry consistently and drawing (a secondary preoccupation throughout his life).
1927-30   Returned to Athens to spend three years in a local tuberculosis sanatorium. His first published poems appeared during these years, and at this time he began studying Marxism and made his lasting commitment to Communism.
1930-31   Entered two sanatoria in Crete, where his disease eventually came under control.
1931-37   Worked in Athens as an actor and dancer with a variety of theatrical groups. Published his first collection, *Tractor*, in 1934, and a second, *Pyramids*, in 1935. His long 1936 poem, *Epitaphios*, appeared in an edition of 10,000 copies, some of which were publicly burned by the Metaxas dictatorship.
1937-38   Spent six months in the Parnitha Sanatorium.
1939-44   Remained in Athens during World War II, largely in bed. Continued to write prolifically.
1945-48   In early January joined the EAM (National Liberation Front) forces in Northern Greece and contributed theatrical works to The Peoples' Theatre of Macedonia, especially in the Kozani region. He returned to Athens in mid-February, after the signing of the Varkiza Agreement. He

remained in Athens for the next three years, working as a copyeditor for the publisher Govostis.

1948-52   Arrested and sent into exile on Limnos, then to prison camps on Macronisos (1949) and finally on Aï Strati (1950). Continued to write poetry, burying it in bottles for safekeeping from the camp guards. His published work was banned in Greece at this time.

1952   Freed to return to Athens, joined the EDA party (United Democratic Left) and worked for the newspaper *Avgi*.

1954   Married Falitsa Georgiadis, a doctor on the island of Samos. Their daughter Eri born in 1955.

1955-67   His work began to appear regularly in Greece, several volumes a year (in 1956 his "Moonlight Sonata" won the National Prize for Poetry) and during 1961-64, three volumes of collected poems were published. Volumes of translations and essays also appeared during this period. Ritsos traveled to Russia and a number of Eastern European countries. His work was widely translated throughout Europe and especially celebrated in France.

1967   Arrested under the Papadopoulos dictatorship and sent to prison camps first on Yiaros and then Leros. His poetry again banned in Greece.

1968   After a month's hospitalization in Athens, sent into exile on Samos, under house arrest at his wife's home.

1970   Returned to Athens late in the year to undergo an operation and remained in residence there.

1971   Published in *Ta Nea Keimena*, though his work was still officially banned.

1972   When censorship was eased, published seven volumes of poems, most of which had been written during his imprisonment and exile. Awarded the Grand International Prize for Poetry at the Knokk-le-Zout Biennale. Elected member of the Meinz Academy of Letters and Science.

1974   International Dimitrov Prize of Bulgaria.

1975   Honorary doctorate, University of Thessaloniki. The Alfred de Vigny Poetry Prize of France. Published fourth volume of collected poems and continued to publish individual volumes at regular intervals.

1976   International Poetry Prize of Etna-Taormina, Sicily.   ◊
1977   Lenin Prize. Elected Member of the Mallarmé Academy.
1978   D.Litt., University of Birmingham. His published work at
       this time consisted of seventy-seven volumes of poems, two
       of plays, one of essays, and ten of translations.

THE LOCKERT LIBRARY OF POETRY IN TRANSLATION

Library of Congress Cataloging in Publication Data

Ritsos, Giannēs, 1909–
  Ritsos in parentheses.

  (The Lockert library of poetry in translation)
  I. Keeley, Edmund.   II. Title.
PA5629.17A24   889'.1'32   78-70317
ISBN 0-691-06397-4
ISBN 0-691-01358-6 pbk.